P9-BJD-809

"Here at Citibank we use the Quick Course® computer training book series for 'just-in-time' job aids—the books are great for users who are too busy for tutorials and training. Quick Course® books provide very clear instruction and easy reference."

Bill Moreno, Development Manager
Citibank
San Francisco, CA

"At Geometric Results, much of our work is PC related and we need training tools that can quickly and effectively improve the PC skills of our people. Early this year we began using your materials in our internal PC training curriculum and the results have been outstanding. Both participants and instructors like the books and the measured learning outcomes have been very favorable."

Roger Hill, Instructional Systems Designer
Geometric Results Incorporated
Southfield, MI

"The concise and well organized text features numbered instructions, screen shots, and useful quick reference pointers, and tips…[This] affordable text is very helpful for educators who wish to build proficiency."

Computer Literacy column
Curriculum Administrator Magazine
Stamford, CT

"I have purchased five other books on this subject that I've probably paid more than $60 for, and your [Quick Course®] book taught me more than those five books combined!"

Emory Majors
Searcy, AR

"I would like you to know how much I enjoy the Quick Course® books I have received from you. The directions are clear and easy to follow with attention paid to every detail of the particular lesson."

Betty Weinkauf, Retired Senior
Mission, TX

QUICK COURSE®

in

MICROSOFT®

WINDOWS® 98

-
-
-
-
-

ONLINE PRESS INC. •

Microsoft® *Press*

PUBLISHED BY
Microsoft Press
A Division of Microsoft Corporation
One Microsoft Way
Redmond, WA 98052-6399

Library of Congress Cataloging-in-Publication Data

Quick Course in Microsoft Windows 98 / Microsoft Corporation.
      p.   cm.
   Includes index.
   ISBN 1-57231-742-6
   1. Microsoft Windows (Computer file)   2. Operating systems
(Computers)   I. Microsoft Corporation.
QA76.76.Q63Q522   1998
005.4'469 - - dc21   98-2767
                                                CIP

Printed and bound in the United States of America.

1 2 3 4 5 6 7 8 9   WCWC   3 2 1 0 9 8

Distributed in Canada by ITP Nelson, a division of Thomson Canada Limited.

A CIP record for this book is available from the British Library.

Microsoft Press books are available through booksellers and distributors worldwide. For further information about international editions, contact your local Microsoft Corporation office, or contact Microsoft Press International directly at fax (425) 936-7329. Visit our Web site at mspress.microsoft.com.

A Quick Course® Education/Training Edition for this title is published by Online Press Inc. For information about supplementary workbooks, contact Online Press Inc. at 14320 NE 21st St., Suite 18, Bellevue, WA, 98007, USA, 1-800-854-3344.

Authors: Christina Dudley and Joyce Cox of Online Press Inc., Bellevue, Washington
Acquisitions Editor: Susanne M. Forderer
Project Editors: Maureen Williams Zimmerman, Anne Taussig

From the publisher

"I love these books!"

I can't tell you the number of times people have said those exact words to me about our new Quick Course® software training book series. And when I ask them what makes the books so special, this is what they say:

- **They're short and approachable, but they give you hours worth of good information.**

  Written for busy people with limited time, most Quick Course books are designed to be completed in 15 to 40 hours. Because Quick Course books are usually divided into two parts—Learning the Basics and Building Proficiency—users can selectively choose the chapters that meet their needs and complete them as time allows.

- **They're relevant and fun, and they assume you're no dummy.**

  Written in an easy-to-follow, step-by-step format, Quick Course books offer stream-lined instruction for the new user in the form of no-nonsense, to-the-point tutorials and learning exercises. Each book provides a logical sequence of instructions for creating useful business documents—the same documents people use on the job. People can either follow along directly or substitute their own information and customize the documents. After finishing a book, users have a valuable "library" of documents they can continually recycle and update with new information.

- **They're direct and to the point, and they're a lot more than just pretty pictures.**

  Training-oriented rather than feature-oriented, Quick Course books don't cover the things you don't really need to know to do useful work. They offer easy-to-follow, step-by-step instructions; lots of screen shots for checking work in progress; quick-reference pointers for fast, easy lookup and review; and useful tips offering additional information on topics being discussed.

- **They're a rolled-into-one-book solution, and they meet a variety of training needs.**

  Designed with instructional flexibility in mind, Quick Course books can be used both for self-training and as the basis for weeklong courses, two-day seminars, and all-day workshops. They can be adapted to meet a variety of training needs, including classroom instruction, take-away practice exercises, and self-paced learning.

Microsoft Press is very excited about bringing you this extraordinary series. But you must be the judge. I hope you'll give these books a try. And maybe the next time I see you, you too will say, "Hey, Jim! I love these books!"

Jim Brown, Publisher
Microsoft Press

Content overview

Content details

Introduction

Those of you who are familiar with the Quick Course series of computer training books know that we usually jump right in and start doing useful work with the software you are learning about. We assume that you already have the program loaded on your computer and that you are ready to get going. This book is no exception. If you are sitting at a computer that is set up to run Microsoft Windows 98, you don't need to read this Introduction; you can skip to Part One and proceed from there. But for those of you who have bought an upgrade version of Windows 98 and are faced with the task of installing it over Windows 95, Windows 3.*x*, or Windows for Workgroups 3.*x*, we'll take a minute or two in this Introduction to demystify the installation process.

Before you purchased Windows 98, we assume you checked out the system requirements, which we'll briefly summarize:

- You need a PC with a 486DX or higher processor that runs at a speed of 66 MHz or higher.

- You should have at least 16 MB of memory (more is better).

- Your hard disk must have around 195 MB of free space (more if you plan on installing many of the optional components).

- You need a CD-ROM drive. (You can pay extra for a set of floppy disks, but if you don't already have a CD-ROM drive, it's worth springing for one. Installing from CD-ROM takes a lot less time, most application programs come on CD-ROM these days, and you get extra components for which there is no room on floppy disks.)

Once you have the Windows 98 CD-ROM in hand, the installation process is relatively painless. Turn on your computer and insert the CD-ROM. What happens next depends on your circumstances:

- If you are upgrading from Windows 95, the setup program on the CD-ROM starts immediately, detects that you are running an older version of Windows, and asks whether you want to upgrade. Click Yes.

- If you are upgrading from Windows 3.*x* or Windows for Workgroups 3.*x*, don't start Windows, but instead type the following at the MS-DOS command prompt and press Enter:

D:\setup (Substitute the drive letter of your CD-ROM drive for *D*.)

The setup program on the CD-ROM prompts you to press Enter to initiate a system check. It then runs ScanDisk to check the integrity of your hard drive and asks what to do if it finds problems. When your hard drive has a clean bill of health, click ScanDisk's Exit button.

Now that you have initiated the process according to your existing version of Windows, you see the Windows 98 Setup screen. A dialog box tells you that the installation process will take 30 to 60 minutes, and prompts you to click Continue. You can then sit back, reading the Setup program's instructions and responding to questions as necessary. During the process, a panel on the left side of the Setup screen tells you the steps involved, which steps have been completed, and an estimate of the time remaining. Periodically, information panels highlight features of Windows 98 you will want to check out when setup is complete. The only part of the process that gets a little tricky is if your computer setup includes older types of hardware, and even then, the Setup program does its best to detect the devices and install the necessary drivers for you. (If you have trouble, you may need to contact the device's manufacturer and ask for Windows 98 drivers and installation instructions.)

With the installation process taken care of, you're ready for the rest of this book, which offers streamlined instruction for the new user. Because Windows 98 makes using the computer quick and easy, we think learning Windows should be quick and easy. Our goal is to help you integrate Windows 98 into your daily work life with as little fuss as possible, so that by the time you finish all the chapters, you can forget about your computer's operating system and focus on getting your job done. Good luck!

PART ONE

LEARNING THE BASICS

In Part One, we show you the techniques you need to be able to find your way around Windows 98. After completing these chapters, you will know enough to put Windows 98 to work on a daily basis. In Chapter 1, you explore the desktop, icons, windows and Help. In Chapter 2, you create a document in WordPad, experiment with multitasking, and then print out your work. Chapter 3 teaches you how to organize your files using several Windows programs. In Chapter 4, we introduce you to Outlook Express, and you try your hand at sending e-mail messages.

1

Introducing Windows 98

We set the stage with a discussion of some important operating-system concepts. Then we start Windows 98 and explore its desktop, icons, and windows. We also explore Windows 98 Help before showing you how to safely shut down your computer.

*Access resources
by double-clicking
icons*

*Manually move and
size windows for the
best view*

*Use buttons to expand and
contract windows and
close programs*

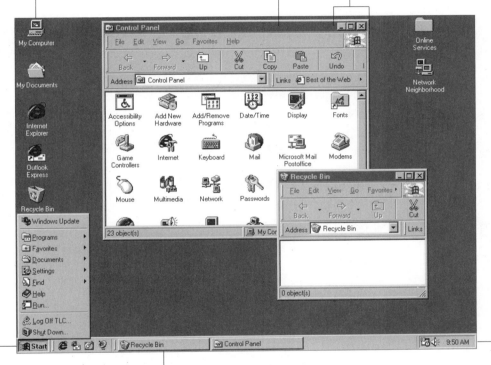

*Access resources by
choosing them from the
Start menu*

*Check the taskbar to
know which programs
are open*

*This end of the
taskbar provides
useful information*

Since the introduction of Microsoft Windows 95, computers have gotten faster, more powerful, and cheaper. Meanwhile, the computing world has gotten broader, with greater emphasis on the Internet. To keep pace with these developments, Microsoft has updated its flagship operating system, not only to improve the existing features of Windows 95 but also to realize the potential of full Internet integration.

Why Do You Need an Operating System?

So what exactly is an operating system and why do you need one? Your computer's operating system coordinates all your *hardware* (the central processing unit or CPU, memory, hard drives, floppy drives, CD-ROM drives, monitor, keyboard, mouse, and any other devices) by means of *software* (computer programs). When you work on your computer, you work with two kinds of software: application programs and system programs.

Hardware ⟶

Software ⟶

- **Application programs.** You use these programs to perform specific types of tasks. For example, you can construct spreadsheet models with spreadsheet programs such as Microsoft Excel, and you can write reports with word-processing programs such as Microsoft Word. On the surface, a spreadsheet program and a word-processing program might seem very different, but these programs share many functions. For example, both need to respond to keyboard instructions, retrieve files from a hard drive or floppy drive, show the information in files on-screen, change the information, and save it on a disk. Each application could provide its own instructions for these routine tasks, but long ago software developers realized it would be more efficient to have one set of system programs carry out these basic functions for all other programs.

- **System programs.** These programs were developed to perform basic computer functions, and a collection of system programs that were designed to work together became known

No Internet Explorer?

If you don't have an Internet Explorer icon on your desktop (see the facing page), you might be working with a version of Windows 98 that does not provide Internet integration. Don't worry. You will still be able to follow along with almost all of our examples, because we don't talk much about the Internet in this book.

as an operating system. By managing files and hardware devices and overseeing basic functions, an operating system provides a foundation for the application programs that are designed to work with or *run under* it. That way, as long as the developers of application programs make sure their programs work with a particular operating system, they don't have to worry about making them work with every kind of CPU, every kind of monitor, every kind of sound card, and so on.

Well, that's enough preamble. You're probably anxious to get started and see what the Windows 98 operating system is all about. Because we assume that Windows 98 is already installed on your computer, we don't go into the details about installation in this book. Instead, we focus on what you need to know about Windows to do useful work. We do give some background information for new computer users, but those of you who are new to Windows but not new to computers can simply skim over those sections. Let's get going.

The Desktop

When you turn on your computer, Windows 98 rushes around setting everything up, and when it's finished, you see a screen that looks something like this one:

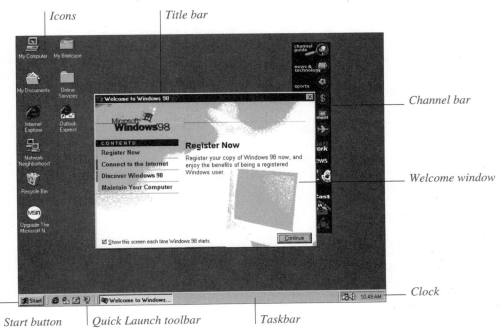

Icons →

The taskbar →

The Windows opening screen is known as the *desktop*. This metaphor is designed to make using the tools available with Windows no more intimidating than using the tools found on a typical desk in a typical office. (If you are already familiar with Windows 95, you'll instantly recognize many of the items on this desktop as the ones used by that operating system.)

The desktop shown on the previous page includes the Welcome window that appears the first time you start Windows 98 after it is installed. (Don't worry if you don't see the Welcome window on your screen.) Also visible are *icons* that represent the Windows tools you will use most frequently. Running horizontally across the bottom of the screen is the *taskbar*, which has a Start button on the left and a clock on the right. Other items displayed on the taskbar depend on your computer's setup and the current task, as you'll see while working through this book. The desktop may also include a Channel bar and a Quick Launch toolbar, which provide easy access to the Internet from the desktop. (Again, don't worry if the Channel bar or the Quick Launch toolbar is missing.)

No taskbar?

If the taskbar is nowhere in sight, you can display it temporarily by pointing to the bottom of your screen. The taskbar will disappear again when you move the pointer. To make the taskbar stay longer, you can press Ctrl+Esc to make the taskbar appear with the Start menu open, and then press Esc to close the Start menu. The taskbar disappears again if you click the desktop. If the taskbar has been moved, you can leave it where it is or, if you like, you can move it by moving the mouse pointer over it, holding down the left mouse button, dragging it to the bottom of the screen, and releasing the mouse button.

Need a password?

When you turn on a computer that is password-protected, you see a box in which you must enter your name and your password. (Windows 98 might enter the name for you.) Once this step is complete, you see the desktop. A computer might be password-protected for three reasons:

- First, you will have to enter a password if the computer is connected to a network.

- Second, you might have to enter a password because a password was specified during the installation of Windows 98. (If your computer is not connected to a network and you want to stop having to enter a password each time you turn on your computer, choose Settings and then Control Panel from the Start menu, double-click Passwords, and click Change Windows Password. Then in the Change Windows Password dialog box, enter your old password, leave the other two boxes blank, click OK twice, and click Close.)

- Third, you will have to enter a password if Windows 98 was set up on your computer with a "user profile" for each person who uses the computer. Windows then sets up the computer according to the specifications in your profile. To find out more about user profiles, double-click the Passwords icon in Control Panel and click the User Profiles tab.

Floating somewhere on the desktop is the *pointer*, which is electronically connected to your mouse. The mouse is essential equipment for working with Windows and the application programs you use. As you move the mouse, the pointer moves correspondingly on the screen, allowing you to point to the item you want to work with. The pointer is often an arrow, but it can take other forms, such as an I-beam when over text or an hourglass when Windows or a program is processing information. When the pointer is where you want it, you can click one of the mouse buttons to activate the item under the pointer, choose a command, and so on; or you can double-click to give other types of instructions. These are the different ways of clicking:

The mouse pointer

- **Clicking.** Clicking is simply a matter of pressing and releasing the primary mouse button once. In this book, we assume that you are using the left mouse button as your primary button and your right mouse button as your secondary button. So when we say *Click the Recycle Bin*, we mean *Move the mouse pointer over the Recycle Bin icon and click the left mouse button once.* If you have reversed the primary and secondary buttons, you would click the right mouse button instead.

- **Right-clicking.** You perform this action by pressing and releasing the secondary mouse button once. When we say *Right-click the desktop*, we mean *Move the pointer to a blank area of the desktop and click the right mouse button.* If you have reversed the buttons, you would click the left mouse button instead.

- **Double-clicking.** To double-click, you quickly click the primary (usually left) mouse button twice.

Before we can explore the desktop, we need to deal with the Welcome window. (If you don't see a Welcome window on your screen, read the following paragraphs but skip the instructions.) You'll do almost all of your work with Windows

Program window instead of desktop?

If you turn on your computer and wind up with a program already started, that program has been added to the StartUp submenu of Programs on the Start menu. You can simply click the Close button (the button with an X) at the right end of the title bar to close the program and display the desktop. Or you can click the Show Desktop button on the Quick Launch toolbar.

Windows

The Close button

ToolTips

in some sort of *window*. In this case, the window displays options for obtaining more information about Windows 98 and for registering the product. Follow these steps to close the window:

1. Move the pointer over to the Close button at the right end of the Welcome window's title bar and notice that Windows displays a pop-up box that shows the name of the button. This handy feature, called *ToolTips*, is prevalent throughout Windows 98.

2. Click the left mouse button once to close the window.

We'll talk more about windows in a moment. But first, we need to make sure we are all looking at the same desktop.

Desktop Variations

Your desktop might look different from ours for a variety of reasons. For example, your computer might have a larger monitor, you might have changed the default screen colors, or you might be working at a different screen resolution. (The resolution of screens in this book is 800 x 600.) Your desktop might also be set to a different style than ours, and the style can affect how the desktop works. So that you can follow along with our examples without any glitches, we all need to set our screens to the same style. To do that, we'll lead you quickly through a series of steps without much explanation. Don't worry if you don't fully understand what's going on at this point: we'll explain things in more detail later. Here goes:

The Start button

1. Point to the Start button at the left end of the taskbar and click to display a list of options.

2. Point to Settings in the list, move the pointer to the right onto the next list that appears, then point to Folder Options, and click. Windows displays the dialog box shown at the top of the facing page.

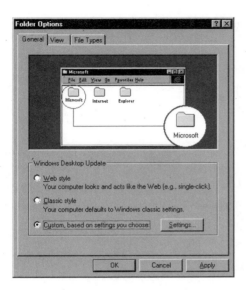

As you can see, you can select Web Style or Classic Style, or you can create a custom style that mixes and matches elements of both styles.

3. Click the circle to the left of Classic Style and then click the word *OK* at the bottom of the dialog box. The dialog box closes and various items disappear, so that you are now looking at a less cluttered desktop.

Working with Icons

The icons on the desktop represent elements of Windows that we will cover later in the book. As you install application programs on your computer, those programs may add icons to the desktop, to the point where your efficiency may suffer because of the clutter. You need to know how to manipulate icons to keep the desktop neat and tidy. Try this:

1. Point to the Online Services icon, hold down the left mouse button, move the pointer to the top right corner of the desktop, and release the button. This hold-move-release action is called *dragging*. As you move the pointer, a shadow image of the Online Services icon moves with it, and when you release the mouse button, the icon jumps to its new location.

Moving icons

Dragging

2. Point to the Network Neighborhood icon, noticing that Windows displays a pop-up box describing the function of the icon.

3. Drag the Network Neighborhood icon below the Online Services icon.

4. Drag the other icons to fill the empty spaces so that your screen looks like this:

5. If you want, move other icons to the right side of the desktop.

You need not worry about aligning your icons precisely, but if you like, follow these steps to nudge the icons into straight lines:

1. Right-click an empty area of the desktop. (Remember, this means click the secondary—usually right—mouse button once.) You see this list:

A list like this one, called a *shortcut menu*, appears whenever you right-click an object. The menu provides easy access to the commands that perform actions commonly associated with the object. (We talk more about menus and commands on page 29; for now, simply follow along.)

Shortcut menus

2. Point to Line Up Icons and click the left mouse button. Windows straightens up the icons in their separate areas on the desktop.

   Suppose you don't like icons scattered around the screen after all. You can simply tell Windows to rearrange them for you. Follow these steps:

1. Right-click the desktop to reopen its shortcut menu and then point to Arrange Icons. Windows then displays a *submenu* like the one shown here:

Submenus

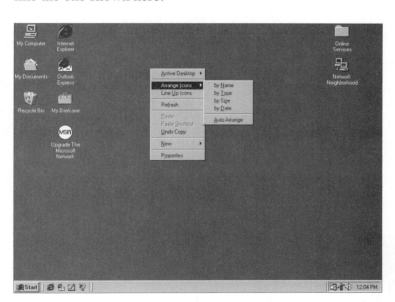

2. Point to By Name and click. Windows realigns all the icons in their original order, reassuming their positions on the left side of the desktop. (Why doesn't Windows 98 put the icons in alphabetic order? The icons Windows creates are moved to their default locations so that they always appear in the same place on the desktop. Any icons you have added are arranged alphabetically.)

Initial capital letters

Sometimes the capitalization of the option names we use doesn't exactly match what's on the screen. We capitalize the first letter of every word to set them off in a sentence. For example, in the adjacent steps, we tell you to click By Name, when the option on the screen is by Name. See what we mean? Our names stand out better, don't they?

If you want Windows to act like a drill sergeant and automatically straighten up the ranks of icons, this is what you do:

Auto-arranging icons

1. Right-click the desktop, point to Arrange Icons, point to Auto Arrange, and then click. Nothing seems to happen, but behind the scenes, Windows is now on duty.

2. Drag the Recycle Bin to the middle of the desktop. When you release the mouse button, the remaining icons move up to fill the Recycle Bin's place, and the Recycle Bin icon snaps back to the left side of the desktop, but at the bottom of the rank.

3. Right-click the desktop, point to Arrange Icons, point to By Name, and click. The default pecking order is restored.

4. Right-click, point to Arrange Icons, point to Auto Arrange, and click to send Windows off-duty. Now you can move the icons wherever you want them.

Being able to shuffle icons on the screen is all well and good, but why are they there? Icons are not just cute little pictures; they represent programs and other computer elements, such as hardware, storage areas, or documents. Double-clicking an icon carries out a specific action, such as starting a program or displaying the contents of a folder. Here's an example:

The Recycle Bin icon

1. Double-click the Recycle Bin icon. This window opens:

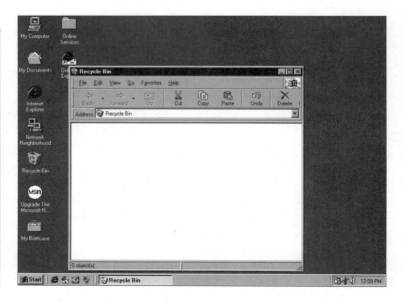

Bold shortcut-menu commands

When you right-click an object on the Windows desktop, you'll often notice that one command on the shortcut menu appears in bold. If you simply double-click the object, the bold command is carried out automatically. For example, when you right-click the Recycle Bin icon, the Open command appears in bold on the shortcut menu. If you double-click the Recycle Bin instead, its window opens automatically.

The Recycle Bin is an area on your hard drive to which files are moved when you "delete" them. Our Recycle Bin is currently empty, but yours may contain deleted items. (See page 86 for information about how to use the Recycle Bin.)

2. Notice that a button representing the Recycle Bin window has appeared on the taskbar at the bottom of the screen. We'll talk more about this button in a moment.

Leave the Recycle Bin window open for now and watch what happens to it as you work through the next section.

Working with the Start Button

An important feature of the desktop is the Start button at the left end of the taskbar. As its name implies, you can start many tasks by clicking this button. Follow these steps:

1. Move the pointer to the Start button at the left end of the taskbar at the bottom of the screen, and click the left mouse button once to display this Start menu:

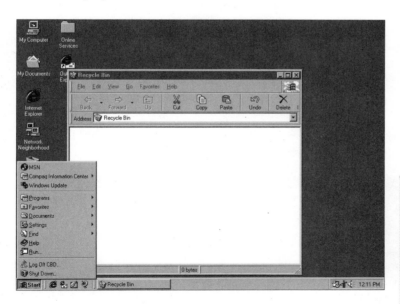

The items on the Start menu are fast ways to carry out common computer tasks, such as starting programs, finding and opening files, changing system settings, and getting information.

Start menu variations

Your Start menu may look different from the one we show, depending on what programs are installed on your computer and whether your Start menu has been customized. For example, if your Start menu has Windows 98 written down the left side, and its icons look larger than our icons, don't worry. Your Start menu is set to show large icons and ours is set to show small icons.

2. Move the pointer to Settings and click so that the Settings sub-menu stays open even if the mouse moves:

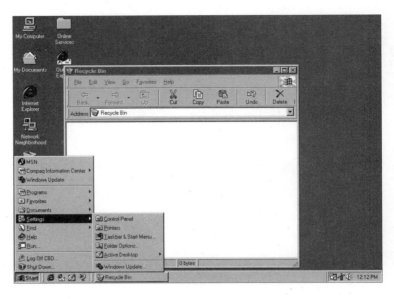

The Control Panel

3. Move the pointer to Control Panel and click. Your desktop now looks like this:

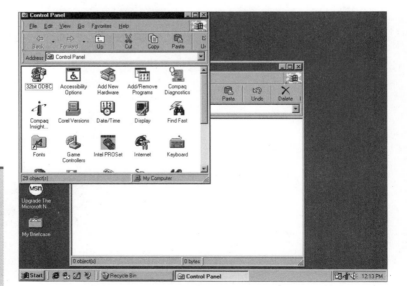

A full taskbar

If you open many windows, the taskbar can get pretty full of buttons. Windows then abbreviates the button names to accommodate them all. If you can't tell which button belongs to which window, point to the button for a brief moment, and the full window name will pop up.

The Control Panel window contains icons representing programs that control various aspects of your computer system. You may have fewer, more, or different icons, depending on your computer setup. We won't explore these icons here. Because the window is not big enough to display all its contents, a scroll bar appears down the right side of the Control Panel window. Don't worry about this for now; we talk about scrolling on page 33.

If you used Windows 95 before upgrading to Windows 98, you may be noticing some differences in the look of the components of the two operating systems. As you can see, the Control Panel and Recycle Bin windows are essentially the same; notice, however, that the Internet's influence on Windows 98 is reflected in the bars at the top of the window. For example, the Go and Favorites menus found in Web browsers have been added to the menu bar, and an Address bar indicates the name of the window you are now looking at and lets you look at other things. You'll see how you can take advantage of these items as you work your way through this book.

Notice that you didn't have to close the Recycle Bin window to open the Control Panel window. Although the Control Panel window obscures the Recycle Bin window, the Recycle Bin is still open, as indicated by the presence of its button on the taskbar.

Window Basics

As the name *Windows 98* implies, when you're working with Windows or one of its programs, you're always working in a window. So while we have these two windows open, let's learn some basic windowing skills before we go any further.

Sizing and Moving Windows

With many programs, you'll want to work in a window that occupies the entire screen so that you can see as much of your work as possible. Sometimes, however, you'll want the window to take up less of the screen so that you can see other items on your desktop. Two buttons clustered with the Close button at the right end of the title bars of most windows allow you to quickly contract and expand the windows. You can also size the windows manually. To try sizing and moving, follow the steps on the next page.

The Maximize button

1. Click the Maximize button on the Control Panel window's title bar. The Restore button replaces the Maximize button, and the window expands to fill the screen, as shown here:

The Restore button

2. Click the Restore button. The window shrinks again, and the Maximize button replaces the Restore button.

Switching windows

3. Click the Recycle Bin button on the taskbar to bring its window to the forefront, like this:

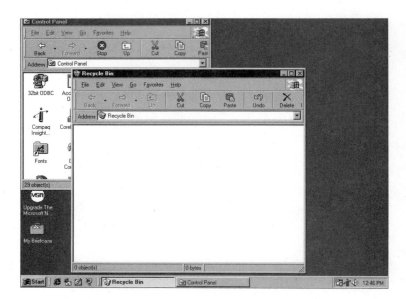

Notice that the title bar of the active window is a brighter color than that of the inactive window. Also notice that the active window's button on the taskbar is lighter in color and appears "pressed."

4. Click the Recycle Bin window's Maximize button to expand the window to fill the screen.

5. Click the Control Panel button on the taskbar to make it the active window.

Except for the windows of some very simple programs, all windows that don't occupy the entire screen have *frames*, and most frames can stretch and shrink. As you move the pointer over different parts of a frame that is resizable, the pointer becomes a two-headed arrow, indicating the directions in which you can move the frame to change its size. You can move the sides of the window frame to the left and right, move the top and bottom of the frame up and down, and move the corners up and down diagonally. Let's experiment:

← **Frames**

1. Point to the right side of the Control Panel window's frame. When the pointer changes to a double-headed arrow, hold down the left mouse button, move the mouse to the right to make the window wider, and release the mouse button.

← **Sizing windows manually**

2. Point to the bottom of the frame and drag it until the window is about 3 inches tall.

3. Point to the diagonal lines in the bottom right corner of the window and drag in any direction to change the window's height and width simultaneously.

4. Point to the window's title bar and drag right, left, up, or down. The window moves to its new location. (You can also move a window using the keyboard; see the tip on page 28.)

← **Moving windows**

5. Now click the Maximize button on the title bar to expand the window so that it fills the screen. The Maximize button is replaced by the Restore button, and the window's frame disappears. (Because a maximized window doesn't have a frame, you can't manually resize it.)

Flipping between Restore and Maximize

When a window is maximized, you can restore it to its previous size by double-clicking its title bar. Double-clicking the title bar of a window that does not fill the screen maximizes the window.

You can shrink the window to its minimum size and tuck it out of sight under its button on the taskbar. Although it's not visible, a minimized window is still accessible, as you'll see if you follow these steps:

The Minimize button

1. Click the Minimize button. The window appears to shrink into its taskbar button, the button turns gray to indicate that its window is inactive. The only other open window, the Recycle Bin, becomes active.

2. Redisplay the Control Panel window by clicking its button on the taskbar.

Arranging Windows

What if you want an unobstructed view of all open windows? You could size each window in turn, but instead, let's try an easier method:

1. Right-click a blank spot at the right end of the taskbar to show this shortcut menu of commands associated with the taskbar:

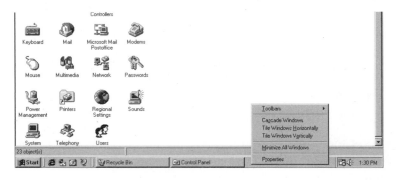

If you right-click the Quick Launch toolbar instead, you see the shortcut menu of taskbar commands shown above with five more commands associated with the Quick Launch toolbar.

2. Click Tile Windows Horizontally.

3. Right-click the taskbar and click Tile Windows Vertically to see that effect. Then right-click the taskbar one more time and click Cascade Windows. The result is shown at the top of the facing page.

Minimized windows are not arranged

If any open programs are minimized or if they have open dialog boxes, their windows are not included in screen rearrangements carried out using the four taskbar commands.

4. After you implement a window arrangement, a command that lets you undo that arrangement is added to the taskbar shortcut menu. To see the effects of this command, right-click the taskbar and click Undo Cascade.

Undoing window arrangements

5. Finally, right-click the taskbar and click Minimize All Windows to tuck both windows under their buttons on the taskbar.

Minimizing all windows

Getting Help

Using Windows 98 is fairly intuitive, and this book will help you find your way around so that, most of the time, you will know exactly what to do and how. However, for those times when you stumble, you'll want to consult Windows 98 Help. Think of Help as an encyclopedia-sized book in which you can look up just about any topic. Windows provides Help topics for all its components, and you access these topics by following these steps:

1. Click the Start button and then click Help on the Start menu to display the window shown on the next page.

Help with programs

Most Windows programs have Help features that function in much the same way as Windows 98 Help. In a program, you can often press the F1 key to instantly access the Help dialog box.

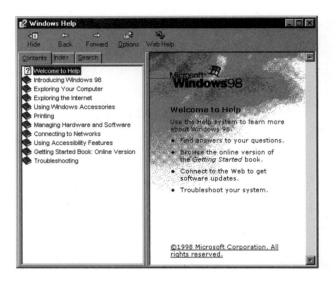

Using the Contents tab

The left pane of the window is multilayered, with each layer designated by a tab, like a manila file folder tab. The Contents tab is currently displayed. (If it's not, click Contents to bring it to the forefront.) This tab organizes Help topics in broad categories.

2. Point to the book icon to the left of *Introducing Windows 98*. Notice that the pointer then changes to a hand icon and that *Introducing Windows 98* changes color and becomes underlined. These changes indicate that the Contents list is actually a series of *hyperlinks* that you can click to jump directly to other places in Help.

Hyperlinks

3. Click the book icon to display a list of available categories.

4. Next, click the book icon to the left of *What's New In Windows 98* to display a list of topics.

5. Click the question-mark icon to the left of *A Faster Operating System* to display the text of this topic in the right pane as shown at the top of the facing page.

Hidden Help information

In some topics, you can click a hyperlink to open the dialog box necessary to complete the task you are inquiring about. At other times, clicking a hyperlinked word displays a pop-up definition of that word. Clicking a *Related Topics* hyperlink displays a pop-up box that lists related topics. You can then click a topic to display its information in the Help window's right pane.

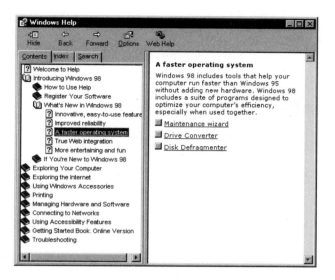

6. In the right pane, click the Disk Defragmenter topic and read the information that appears below the topic.

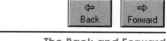

The Back and Forward buttons

7. To hide the information, click the Back button on the toolbar. Then to reopen the topic, click the Forward button. (See the tip below for more information about the Help toolbar.)

In addition to clicking topics on the Contents tab, you can search for specific information by following these steps:

1. Click the Index tab. The left pane of the window changes to display an alphabetic list.

Using the Index tab

2. Type *shut* in the edit box above the list of topics. The list box scrolls to the topics that start with those letters.

3. With *shutting down* highlighted, click the Display button to see this list of related topics:

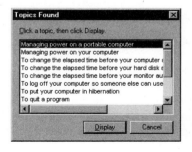

The Help toolbar

You can click the Options button to show a drop-down menu of commands to go backward or forward, to refresh the page, to stop searching for or loading information, and to print. To close the left pane so that only the right pane is displayed, click the Hide button. To redisplay both panes, click the Show button. If you have Internet access, you can click the Web Help button to get help from Microsoft's Web site. (See the tip on the next page.)

4. Press the Down Arrow key on your keyboard repeatedly, until the next-to-last item in the topics list, *To shut down your computer*, is selected. Then click Display to display instructions in the window's right pane, as shown here:

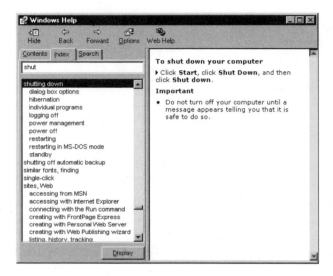

5. Close the window by clicking its Close button.

Using the Search tab

As you feel more comfortable working with the Help window, you might want to try using the Search tab, which searches the full text of the topics to find a word or words you enter, instead of relying only on topic headings. Simply click the Search tab, type a word or two about your topic in the Keyword edit box, and click the List Topics button. You can then select a topic and click Display.

You might want to explore the Windows 98 Help feature on your own for a while. When you have finished, you should

Using the Web for help

When you click the Web Help button in the Windows Help dialog box, Windows displays information about Microsoft's technical-support service, Support Online. Click the *Support Online* hyperlink to open Internet Explorer, which takes you to a Microsoft Web page that displays Windows Update. Click Connect when Windows asks you to connect to your Internet Service Provider (ISP). (You will have to register with the site the first time you use Support Online.) With Windows Update, you can seek technical support, report problems, and keep your system current by downloading updates from the Web site. As an alternate method for accessing Windows Update, click the Start button and choose Windows Update from the Start menu.

rejoin us as we take you through the steps for turning off your computer.

Shutting Down Your Computer

Well, this section is going to be easy, because you've already learned from Windows 98 Help how to turn off your computer. A word of warning: never flip your computer's on/off switch without running through the shut-down procedure. Windows does a lot of housekeeping at the end of each session to ensure that your computer will function properly the next time you turn it on. If you simply flip the switch, none of the housekeeping gets done, and there's no telling how future sessions might be affected. Here's how to shut down correctly:

◄──────────────────────────

WARNING!

1. Click the Start button and then click Shut Down. (It doesn't make sense to stop from the Start menu but you'll get used to it.) Windows displays the Shut Down Windows dialog box:

You can also hold down the Alt key and press F4 to display this dialog box, which contains a set of options that are fairly self-explanatory. (See the adjacent tip for information about the Stand By option.)

2. If necessary, click Shut Down to select it, and then click OK. Windows records information about this session, including the fact that the Recycle Bin and Control Panel windows are minimized on the taskbar. Then it displays a message telling you that you can turn off your computer.

3. Turn everything off.

Well, that's it for the quick tour. In the next chapter, we'll focus on running programs.

Standing by

Your computer can temporarily turn off its monitor and hard disks when it is idle if you tell it to stand by. Before switching to Stand By mode, you should save your work. Then, leaving any open or minimized program windows as they are, choose Shut Down from the Start menu, select the Stand By option, and click OK. When you want to resume your work, simply press the Spacebar. Windows wakes up with all the program windows open or minimized as you left them.

2

Using Programs

While using WordPad to create a document, we discuss how to start programs and choose commands using menus and toolbar buttons. Then we start a couple of other programs to demonstrate multi-tasking and show how to print files.

*Choose commands
from menus or use
toolbar buttons*

*Manipulate all program,
folder, and document
windows the same way*

*Recycle information by
copying and pasting it
between programs*

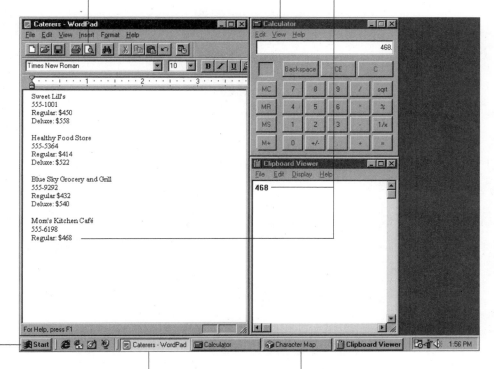

*Start programs by
choosing them from
the Start menu*

*Switch among programs
by clicking their taskbar
buttons*

*Display invisible but
open programs with a
simple mouse click*

If you are like most computer users, you aren't interested in computers and their software for their own sakes. You want to do useful work. You want to send a letter, jot down notes for a meeting, draft a report, or analyze your income and expenses for the month. So the first thing you want to know about Windows 98 is how to start programs and how to create, save, and print documents. By the time you finish this chapter, you'll have enough information to be able to use your own programs to carry out your daily tasks. (We don't talk about adding and removing programs in this chapter.)

Assuming that you shut down your computer at the end of Chapter 1, the first thing you need to do is turn on your computer. Notice that Windows 98 remembers that the Recycle Bin and the Control Panel were open when you shut down your computer, and it displays their windows when it starts up. (Windows does this for some of its own programs, but it does not reopen applications like word processors at startup unless they are listed on the StartUp submenu.)

Starting Programs

One of the simplest ways to get going is to start a program from the Start menu. (*Starting a program* is also referred to as *running*, *executing*, *launching*, or *loading a program*. Generally, these terms can be used interchangeably.) Try this:

1. Minimize both Control Panel and the Recycle Bin, and then click the Start button at the left end of the taskbar to display the Start menu shown on page 13.

2. Move the pointer to Programs and click. Windows displays a submenu of programs and program groups. Clicking a program name starts that program, and moving the pointer to a program group displays yet another submenu.

3. Move the pointer to Accessories at the top of the Programs submenu. Windows displays another submenu that lists the programs and program groups that are in the Accessories program group. Your screen now looks something like this:

Starting MS-DOS programs

If you still work with some MS-DOS programs or prefer to use some MS-DOS commands, you can still access a version of the old operating system while working in Windows 98. To start MS-DOS, choose Programs and then MS-DOS Prompt from the Start menu. (If you want to see your desktop while working in MS-DOS, press Alt+Enter to switch from full-screen mode to window mode.) Then you can run programs and give commands in the familiar way. For example, to start the MS-DOS Editor program, simply type *edit* at the command prompt and press Enter. (Under Windows 98, MS-DOS Editor has a menu bar with commands that make working with files easier, so to quit the program, simply choose Exit from the File menu.) To quit MS-DOS Prompt, type *exit* at the command prompt and press Enter. To start an MS-DOS program without going through MS-DOS Prompt, choose Run from the Start menu, type the program's file name in the Open edit box, and click OK.

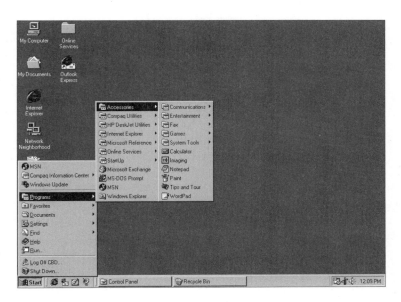

4. Move the pointer onto the Accessories submenu and then to WordPad, and click to start the WordPad program, a simple word processor that comes with Windows 98. After Windows starts WordPad, you see the window below on your screen. (Don't worry if your window is a different size than ours.)

Starting WordPad

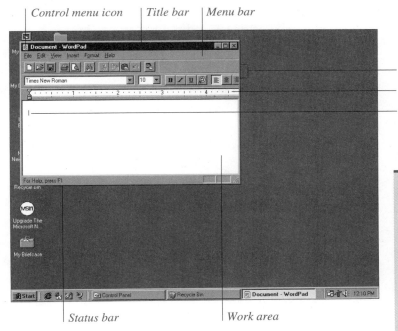

Control menu icon | Title bar | Menu bar

Toolbars
Ruler
Insertion point

Status bar | Work area

Programs submenu variations

The Programs submenu in our illustration is for a new computer on which no application programs have been installed. When you install an application, its installation program might add an item or a group to the Programs submenu.

Notice that a button representing the WordPad window has been added to the taskbar.

Quitting programs from the taskbar

5. Right-click the Recycle Bin button on the taskbar and then click Close in the shortcut menu. Repeat this step for the Control Panel button.

6. Maximize the WordPad window.

Anatomy of a program window

The window now on your screen has many of the characteristics of program windows. It has a *title bar*, which in this case tells you that the window contains a WordPad document. Below the title bar is a *menu bar*, which lists the command menus available for WordPad. Below the menu bar are one or two *toolbars*, which are collections of buttons that you can click to quickly carry out often-used commands. (We'll talk about the various ways of giving commands in a moment.) Below them, you might see a *ruler*, a handy measuring tool that helps you design more complicated documents. At the bottom of the window is a *status bar*, where the program posts various items of useful information. Occupying the majority of the window is a *work area*, where you create your document. In this area, a blinking *insertion point* indicates where the next character you type will appear. (Don't confuse the insertion point with the pointer, which moves with your mouse and doesn't blink.)

Back to the title bar. At the left end is the *Control menu icon*. Clicking this icon displays a menu of commands for sizing and moving the window and quitting the program. (You can also carry out these commands in other, simpler ways.) At the right end of the title bar are the same Minimize, Maximize/Restore, and Close buttons you used in Chapter 1.

The WordPad program is very simple and can handle only one document at a time. With more sophisticated programs, you can open two or more documents; in this case, each document is displayed in its own document window within the program window. Document windows have only title bars—no menu bars, toolbars, or status bars. Here's what the screen looks like when two documents are open in Word 97:

Moving windows with the keyboard

Sometimes a window can slide inexplicably so far off the screen that you can't grab its title bar and drag it back. If that happens, you can move the window by pressing Alt+Spacebar (the equivalent of clicking the Control menu icon), choosing Move from the Control menu, using the Arrow keys to bring the title bar into view, and pressing Enter.

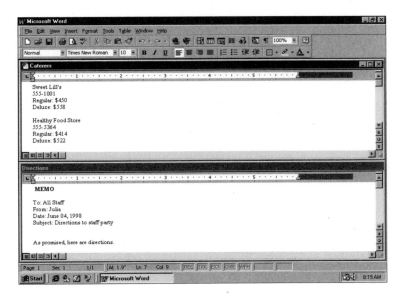

The program window's title bar now displays only the program name, and the document windows' title bars display the names of the documents the windows contain. On the taskbar, the program's button displays the name of the program. (Document windows don't get their own buttons.)

Command Basics

To get any useful work done, you have to be able to tell the computer what to do. Windows and the programs you run under Windows provide a number of methods for giving instructions. We'll look at the primary methods in this section.

Choosing Commands from Menus

You've already seen the Start menu and know that it's just a list of tasks you might want to perform, including starting a program. Here, we'll look at a couple of other kinds of menus.

Using Menus on the Menu Bar

In most Windows programs, you usually carry out tasks by choosing commands from the menus listed on the menu bar at the top of the program window. You click the name of the menu you want, and the menu drops down, displaying its list of commands. As part of the effort to give all Windows

Sizing and moving document windows

You can size a document window like a regular window, except that a document window cannot be bigger than its program window. You can also move a document window around, but only within the frame of its program window. When you minimize a document window in some programs, the program shrinks the window under a small title bar at the bottom of the program window. To redisplay the window, double-click this title bar.

Menu standardization →

programs a common look, menus with commands that carry out similar tasks often have the same names and occupy the same position on the menu bar in different programs. The File menu and Help menu are two such common menus. For example, the File menu usually contains commands such as New (for creating new items such as documents), Open (for opening existing documents), Save (for saving the current document), and Exit (for leaving the program). This menu always appears at the left end of the menu bar.

To choose a command from a menu, you simply click the command. To close a menu without choosing a command, you either click an empty spot away from the menu or press the Esc key. Let's take a look at a few menus and choose a command or two:

Dropping down a menu →

1. Click the word *File* on the menu bar to drop down the File menu shown here:

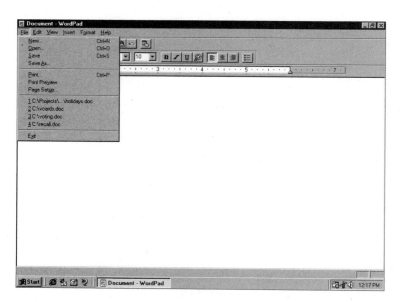

All Windows programs present their menu commands in consistent ways and use the following visual cues to tell you various things about the commands:

Help with commands

After dropping down a menu, you can point to a command to display a description of its function in the program's status bar.

- **Groups.** Commands that perform related tasks are grouped, and the group is separated from other commands by a line.

- **Unavailable commands.** Some commands appear in gray letters, indicating they are not currently available. For example, many programs have Cut and Copy commands on their Edit menus that appear in gray letters until something has been selected in the active document that can be cut or copied.

- **Dialog boxes.** Some commands are followed by an ellipsis (...), indicating that you must supply information in a special kind of window called a dialog box before the command can be carried out. (More about dialog boxes in a moment.)

- **Keyboard shortcuts.** Key combinations appear to the right of some commands, indicating that you can bypass the menu and carry out the command by pressing the corresponding keyboard shortcut.

- **Submenus.** Some command names are followed by a triangle, indicating that the command has a submenu. (You saw how submenus work when you started WordPad.)

- **Toggles.** Some commands are preceded by a check mark, indicating that you can "toggle" the command on and off.

  The commands on the File menu illustrate three of the visual cues in this list.

2. Now move the pointer over the word *View* on the menu bar to drop down that menu. (Notice that once one menu is open, you don't have to click to open another.)

3. Move the pointer down to Ruler, which is a toggle command, and click to choose the command. If the ruler was turned on, it is now turned off; if it was turned off, it is now turned on.

4. Click View on the menu bar to display the View menu again, and notice whether the Ruler command is preceded by a check mark to indicate that it is turned on. If it is, press the Esc key to close the menu; if it isn't, choose Ruler to turn on the command and redisplay the ruler.

5. If the format bar does not appear in the WordPad window, choose Format Bar from the View menu to turn it on.

Choosing commands with the keyboard

To use keyboard shortcuts to choose commands, you need to memorize the shortcuts. If you find it faster to use the keyboard but you don't want to tax your memory with key combinations, you can activate the menu bar by pressing Alt and then open the menu you want by pressing the underlined letter in the menu name. Next, choose a command by pressing the underlined letter in the command name. If you change your mind, press Esc to close a menu without choosing a command, and press Esc again to deactivate the menu bar. Once you learn the letters for menus and commands, you can type the key sequence quickly to choose the command. For example, to quit many programs, you can press Alt, then F, and then X.

Using Dialog Boxes

As you saw in Chapter 1, dialog boxes are Windows' way of allowing you to give information or select from several options so that a particular command can be carried out exactly the way you want it. To demonstrate, let's create a memo:

1. Type *MEMO* and press Enter twice.

2. Next, type *To: All Staff*, press Enter, type *From: Julia*, press Enter, and then type *Date:* and a space.

Inserting the date ➤ 3. To insert the date in your memo, choose the Date And Time command from the Insert menu by clicking Insert on the menu bar to display the menu's list of commands (in this case, the objects that can be inserted in a WordPad document) and then clicking Date And Time. WordPad checks your computer for the current date and time and then displays the date and time in various formats in this dialog box:

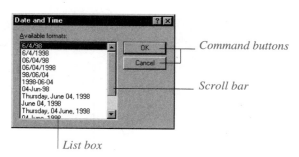

Command buttons

Scroll bar

List box

Correcting mistakes

If you make a mistake while typing the memo, the simplest way to correct it is to press the Backspace key until you have erased the error and then retype the text correctly. If you need to move the insertion point to correct an error, point to the place in the existing text where you want the insertion point to appear and then click the left mouse button. Or you can use the Arrow keys to move the insertion point anywhere in the existing text.

The dialog box is very simple and presents only one set of options, but as you saw when you displayed the Folder Options dialog box in the previous chapter (see page 9), dialog boxes can be pretty complex, with options arranged on tabs. In this particular dialog box, you indicate the format you want for the date by selecting the format from a list box. The list of possible formats is too long to fit in its box, so a scroll bar appears down the right side, allowing you to scroll the list up and down to bring out-of-sight options into view. (See the tip on the facing page for more information about scroll bars.)

4. Click the arrowhead, called a *scroll arrow*, at the bottom of the scroll bar on the right side of the list box to see the other available date and time options.

5. Click the format that is the equivalent of June 04, 1998 to select it. Windows indicates your selection by changing it to white type on a dark background, or *highlighting* it.

6. Click OK. WordPad inserts the current date in the memo in the selected format.

7. Next, press Enter and type *Subject: Directions to staff party*.

8. Press Enter three times and type the following note, pressing Enter where indicated:

   As promised, here are directions to Adventure Works. See you all there on July 4!

   (Press Enter twice.)

   1. Take I-5 North to Alderfield. (Press Enter.)
   2. Take Exit 217 and turn right onto Route 24. (Press Enter.)
   3. Follow the road up-hill and down-dale for 7 miles, until you see the Alpine Ski Center on your left. (Press Enter.)
   4. Turn right onto Park Road, and the entrance to the park is immediately on the left by the totem pole. (Press Enter.)

   When you finish typing, you see the results shown here:

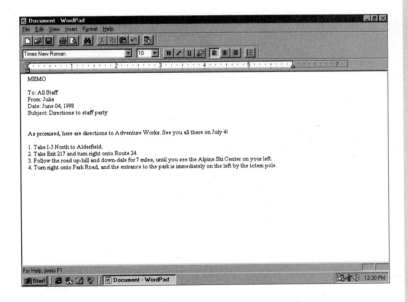

← Selecting an option

Scrolling

When a list box or window is not big enough to show all of its contents, Windows provides vertical and horizontal scroll bars so that you can bring other parts of the contents into view. You can use the vertical scroll bar to move the contents up and down and the horizontal scroll bar to move the contents from side to side. Manipulating scroll bars is an important way of getting around in Windows programs. You can use a couple of scrolling methods. Clicking the arrow at either end of a scroll bar moves the contents a line or a column at a time, whereas clicking on either side of the scroll box on the scroll bar moves the contents a "windowful" at a time. You can also drag the scroll box. The position of the scroll box in relation to the scroll bar tells you where you are in the contents. For example, when the scroll box is in the middle of its bar, the window is positioned roughly halfway through its contents. The size of the scroll box tells you about how much of the contents you can see at one time. For example, if the scroll box is half the length of the scroll bar, you can see half the contents. You can alter the width of the scroll bar by selecting Scrollbar in the Item box on the Appearance tab of the Display Properties dialog box and changing its Size setting. (To open the Display Properties dialog box, right-click the desktop and choose Properties from the shortcut menu.)

Saving documents ────────►

Now let's save the document. In the process, you'll use a more complex dialog box to assign a file name to the document, specify where to store it, and create a folder to hold this and related documents. You'll also get an idea of how your computer's storage (the electronic equivalent of a filing cabinet) is structured. Here we go:

1. Choose the Save As command from the File menu. WordPad displays the Save As dialog box shown here:

All Windows dialog boxes request information in consistent ways and, like commands, use visual cues to let you know the kind of information they need and how you should give it. Here's a list of the most common dialog box components:

- **Edit boxes.** You enter variable information, such as a file name, by typing it in an edit box, represented in the Save As dialog box by the File Name box. If you want to replace an existing entry in an edit box, select the entry and overtype the old text with the new. (See the tip on page 39 for information about selecting.)

- **Spinners.** If an edit box can contain only a number, it sometimes has a pair of up and down arrowheads, called spinners, at its right end. You change the entry either by selecting the existing number and typing a new one or by clicking one of the arrowheads to increase or decrease the number.

- **Sliders.** Number settings can also be represented by the position of a slider on a horizontal or vertical bar. To change the setting, you drag the slider.

Why do you have to save documents?

Your documents exist only in the computer's memory until you save them on a disk. Memory is temporary and can be erased deliberately by turning off your computer and accidentally by power surges and failures. Disk storage is more permanent and can be erased only by using specific commands or due to (fairly rare) drive failures. If all you want to do is type a letter, print it, and send it, you may not need to store an electronic file of the letter on your hard drive. However, you'll want to save the file if you need an electronic record of what the letter said for future reference, if you want to use that letter as the basis for another letter, or if composing the letter is taking a while and you don't want to have to start over in the event of a computer glitch. The hard drives of the world are full of trivial documents that will never again see the light of day and that are not critical to "who said what to whom and when" audit trails. Your company may have a policy about what documents need to be saved and for how long. Otherwise, you can decide for yourself which documents to save.

- **List boxes.** When you need to select from several options, the options are often displayed in list boxes, and when more choices are available than can fit in the list box, the list box has a scroll bar. For example, the list box in the Date And Time dialog box (see page 32) presented a vertical list of options with a vertical scroll bar. Regardless of the format of a list box, you select a listed option by clicking it. The option is then highlighted in the list.

- **Drop-down list boxes.** For space reasons, options are sometimes displayed in drop-down list boxes. Initially, a drop-down list appears as a box containing an option. At the right end of the box is a down arrowhead that you can click to drop down a list of other available options. To select an option, you simply click it. That option then appears in the collapsed list box. The Save As Type option at the bottom of the Save As dialog box is an example of a drop-down list box.

- **Combo boxes.** Sometimes an edit box and a drop-down list box are combined to form a combo box. You can either type in the information needed or you can select it from a drop-down list.

- **Check boxes.** Some options are presented with check boxes (small squares) in front of them. Clicking an empty check box selects the associated option; a ✔ appears in the box to indicate that the option is active, or turned on. Clicking the box again removes the ✔ to indicate that the option is inactive, or turned off. Check boxes operate independently, so if a dialog box presents a group of check boxes, you can select none, one, some, or all of the options, as required for the task at hand.

- **Option buttons.** Other options are presented with option buttons (small circles). There are no option buttons in the dialog box now on your screen, but as you'll see later, these buttons always appear as a group of mutually exclusive options. When you click an option button, a • appears in the button to indicate that the option is active. Because only one option in the group can be active at a time, the • disappears from the button of the previously active option.

Using the keyboard with dialog boxes

In some dialog boxes that require you to type information in edit boxes, it is often quicker to move around the dialog box using the keyboard than to constantly be switching between the keyboard and the mouse. You can move among the elements of a dialog box by pressing the Tab key. (If an edit box is active, it contains a blinking insertion point or a highlighted entry. Otherwise, the active element is designated by a dotted box.) With a list box or a group of option buttons, pressing Tab takes you to the active option. You can then press the Arrow keys to move through the options one at a time, press Home or End to move to the first or last option, or press Page Up or Page Down to display the previous or next boxful of options. When the option you want is selected, press Tab to move to the next element. No matter which element is active, pressing Enter immediately implements the command button that is surrounded by a heavy border. (If a command button is active, you can also implement it by pressing the Spacebar.) At any time, you can press the Esc key to implement the Cancel button.

- **Command buttons.** Most dialog boxes have at least two command buttons: one that closes the dialog box and carries out the command and another one that closes the dialog box and cancels the command. Some dialog boxes have additional command buttons, which you can use to refine the original command. As with commands on menus, if the label on a button is followed by an ellipsis (...), clicking the button opens another dialog box. One command button (in this case, Save) usually has a heavy border around it to indicate that you can press Enter at any time to implement that button.

- **Toolbar buttons.** Some dialog boxes have toolbar buttons that let you interrupt the current task and carry out a different one, or modify the current task in some way. In the Save As dialog box, the five buttons to the right of the Save In edit box are examples of this type of button.

In the Save As dialog box now on your screen, WordPad suggests *Document* as the name of the document in the File Name edit box. The Save In option at the top of the dialog box indicates that WordPad will save your document in the My Documents folder unless you specify otherwise. The list box below gives information about any files already stored in the My Documents folder. Take our word for it: saving a document with a generic name is a bad practice (see page 75). Instead, you want to give the document a unique descriptive name and tuck it in a predictable location with other related documents so that it will be easy to find weeks or even months from now. Continue with these steps:

2. The word *Document* is selected in the File Name box, so simply type *Directions* to replace it. (You can enter information in an edit box only if a blinking insertion point or a highlighted entry tells you the box is active.)

3. Click the arrow to the right of the Save In box to drop down the hierarchical list of potential storage locations, as shown on the facing page.

Paths

Some dialog boxes, such as the one that appears when you choose Run from the Start menu, ask for the path of a program or file. You can think of the path as the file's address. For files stored on your computer, this address starts with the drive letter and traces through folders and subfolders to the file, separating each storage level from the previous one with a backslash (\). For example, C:\Staff Party\Directions is the path of the Directions document stored in the Staff Party folder on your C drive. If you are working on a network, the path of a document stored on another networked computer often starts with two backslashes and the computer name, followed by the drive letter, any folders and subfolders, and the document's file name. When a dialog box requires that you enter a path, you can either type the path directly in the edit box, or if you are unsure of the path (or are a poor typist), you can usually click a Browse button. In the Browse dialog box, you can navigate visually to the file of the program you want to run and then click Open to insert the path of the selected file in the edit box, just as if you had typed it.

The desktop has these storage locations: My Documents (the default document storage folder), My Computer (your PC), and Network Neighborhood (the PCs on any network to which you are connected). It also has Online Services, a folder that contains links to major online services (see the tip on page 94), and may have My Briefcase, a special area used to update files that you work with on another computer, such as a laptop (see page 82). My Computer, in turn, has several storage locations, which, depending on your particular hardware configuration, might consist of floppy drives, hard drives, and CD-ROM drives. If you are connected to a network, Network Neighborhood might have several storage locations as well, depending on which other computers are available to you. (We talk more about storage on page 56.)

Storage locations

4. Click (C:), which designates the main hard drive in your computer. (C:) replaces My Documents in the Save In box, and the list box below it changes to display a set of folders in which various files are already stored on your C drive. (Your list will look different from the one shown in our illustrations because it reflects the folders and files on your C drive.)

You could save the memo directly on your C drive, but it's not a good idea. You wouldn't throw all your paper documents in one big pile if you expected to be able to easily find a specific document later. Instead, you'd organize the documents into categories and store them in file folders or something similar. Likewise, you need to somehow organize your computer documents for easy retrieval.

Name conventions

File names and folder names cannot have more than 255 characters, and they cannot contain these characters:

\ / : * ? " < > |

See page 75 for more advice about naming files and folders.

The Create New Folder button

5. Click the Create New Folder button at the top of the dialog box to create a new folder on your C drive, as shown here:

6. The title of the new folder is highlighted to indicate that it is selected. Type *Staff Party* to replace the selected title with a more descriptive one, and press Enter.

Opening a folder

7. Now double-click the folder icon to the left of Staff Party to open the folder. Staff Party replaces (C:) in the Save In edit box, and the list box is now empty because nothing is stored in the new folder yet.

Selecting a format

8. Click the arrow to the right of the Save As Type option and select Rich Text Format (RTF) from the drop-down list.

9. Click the Save command button to save the memo in Rich Text Format in the Staff Party folder with the name Directions. The dialog box closes, and you return to the WordPad window, where Directions has replaced Document in the title bar and on the taskbar button.

Rich Text Format

You save a document as a Rich Text Format (RTF) file when you don't know which word processor will be used to open it. In an RTF file, the formatting is translated into codes that can be interpreted by most word processors. Even if you open the RTF file in another word processor, such as Word, you will still be able to open it in WordPad.

Changing your mind

If you change your mind about the settings you have made in an open dialog box but you can't remember what the settings were when you started, you can click Cancel or press Esc to close the dialog box. Then all of your changes are discarded and the previous settings remain in effect. You can then start all over if necessary.

Message boxes

Windows programs display message and warning boxes when a command you have chosen can't be carried out or there is a chance you might regret the choice (for example, when you delete files). You can click OK or Yes to acknowledge the message and continue the command. Click Cancel or No to close the message box and cancel the command.

Using Shortcut Menus

Windows programs make extensive use of shortcut menus. As you have seen, these menus group together the commands you are most likely to use with a particular object. An object can be anything from an icon on the desktop to a toolbar in a program window to a word in a document. Let's explore shortcut menus a little further:

1. Choose the Select All command from the Edit menu to select the entire memo.

Selecting the entire document

2. Move the pointer over the selection and click the right mouse button to display this shortcut menu, which includes commands for manipulating the selected text:

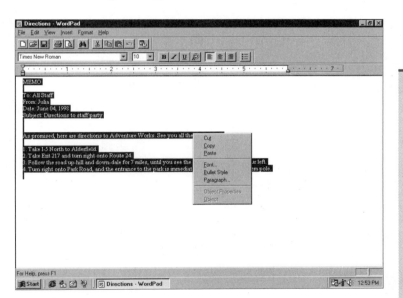

3. Choose Paragraph to display this dialog box:

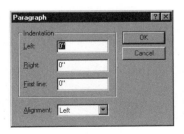

Selecting text

With Windows programs, you can use several techniques for selecting text. (Some programs add a few methods of their own, but we won't go into those here.) You can double-click a word to select it. You can point to the beginning of a block of text, hold down the left mouse button, and drag through the block, releasing the mouse button when the entire block is highlighted. You can click to place an insertion point at the beginning of a block, hold down the Shift key, point to the end of the block, and click to select the words between the two clicks. (This action is sometimes called *shift-clicking*.) Finally, you can click an insertion point, hold down the Shift key, and press an Arrow key, releasing both keys when the text you want is highlighted.

4. Type *1* to replace the highlighted 0 in the Left edit box, and then click the OK command button. Here's the result:

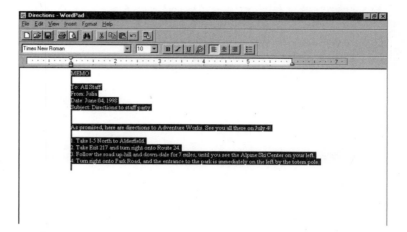

Choosing Commands with Toolbar Buttons

Buttons vs. commands

Many Windows programs come with toolbars, which sport buttons and boxes that carry out common commands. Clicking a button carries out its command with the predefined, or default, settings. When you want something other than its default settings, you must choose the command from its menu. To familiarize yourself with the buttons on the WordPad toolbars, try this:

1. Point to each toolbar button in turn, pausing until the button's name appears in a box below the pointer. This is another demonstration of ToolTips, the feature we mentioned in Chapter 1.

2. Look at the status bar, where WordPad displays a brief description of the button you are pointing to.

To demonstrate how to use toolbar buttons, we'll show you a very important button. The 1-inch left indent you just set looks a bit goofy. You could repeat the previous set of steps to reverse the Paragraph command, but here's an easier way:

The Undo button

1. Click the Undo button on the first toolbar (the equivalent of choosing the Undo command from the Edit menu). WordPad resets the left indent to 0.

Many Windows programs include an Undo feature, enabling you to reverse your last editing action. Knowing that you can always take a step backward makes experimenting less hazardous. It's worth checking out the Undo feature of any program you use so that you know exactly what to do if you paint yourself into a corner. (See the tip below.)

2. Move the pointer to the left of *MEMO* at the top of the document, and when the pointer changes to a right-pointing arrow, click the left mouse button to select just that line.

The Align Right button

3. Click the Align Right button on the format bar (the second toolbar). The line jumps to the right side of the screen, and WordPad changes the look of the button on the format bar so that it appears "pressed." (Looking at the buttons on the format bar is a good way of telling at a glance what formatting is applied to selected text.)

4. Click the Undo button to move the line back to the left side of the screen. Now the Align Left button appears pressed.

The Bold button

5. Click the Bold button on the format bar to make the text bold, and then click a blank area of the document to see this result:

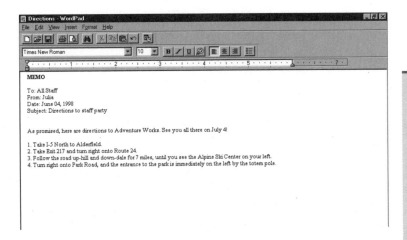

Undo variations

The Undo button can remember only a certain number of changes and can undo most, but not all, actions. Its capabilities vary from program to program, so experiment with less critical documents or save often so that you can backtrack. If Undo does not return your text to the desired formatting, you can always reselect the text and apply the formatting manually using either buttons on a formatting toolbar or commands on the Format menu.

6. Reselect MEMO and try clicking other buttons on the format bar and then clicking Undo. When you are ready, click the

The Save button

Save button to save the document with the current settings in the Save As dialog box, including the file name.

For practice, you might want to create a new document (see the facing page) and experiment with formatting commands.

Multitasking

The term *multitasking* might sound intimidating, but the concept is simple: multitasking is carrying out two or more tasks at the same time. For example, you might be writing a report while your computer is printing another document, or while your communications program is downloading information from an online service, or while your e-mail program is receiving an incoming message. In practice, most people don't often take advantage of multitasking. They usually open two or three programs and work with one while the others sit idly in memory, waiting until they are needed. The programs have been started and they are available, but they aren't actually doing any work.

Having several programs open at once saves you time by allowing you to keep all the information you need at your fingertips, whether it is stored in a report, in a spreadsheet, in a database, or in any other type of document. If you're in the middle of writing a letter and need to look up some figures in a spreadsheet, you no longer have to stop what you are doing, quit the word processor, load the spreadsheet, find the figures, and then start your word processor again. You can simply flip between windows to get the information you need.

Foreground vs. background

Although you can have more than one program running at the same time, only one program can run *in the foreground*, meaning that its window is active and receiving input from you. Any other open program runs *in the background*, meaning that it is behind the scenes, either carrying out some prescribed task or waiting for your next instruction. Let's use the keyboard to start another program and experiment:

Starting Calculator

1. Hold down the Ctrl key and press Esc to open the Start menu, press the Up Arrow key until Programs is highlighted, and then press Enter. The Programs submenu opens with Accessories selected.

2. Press Enter to open the Accessories submenu, press the Down Arrow key until Calculator is selected, and press Enter to start the mini number cruncher that comes with Windows:

3. Click anywhere in the WordPad window to bring it to the foreground and make it active.

4. Click the New button and when WordPad asks you to specify a format for the new document, double-click Rich Text Document to both select that option and implement the default command button (the one with the heavy border).

The New button

Switching Among Running Programs

As you just saw, it's easy to switch to a program when you can see part of its window. If you are working in a maximized window and can't see the windows of programs running in the background, you can use the taskbar buttons to switch programs. As a demonstration, suppose you are responsible for providing appetizers for the staff party, and while browsing through the Yellow Pages, you use WordPad to take down information about potential caterers. Follow these steps:

1. In the new document, type *Sweet Lill's* and press Enter.

2. Type *555-1001*, and press Enter twice.

Two identical buttons on the taskbar?

If two identical program buttons are displayed on the taskbar, it means you have started the same program twice. Unless you have started them intentionally, you should close one of the copies to avoid confusion.

3. Add these caterers to the list:

   Healthy Food Store (Press Enter.)
   555-5364 (Press Enter twice.)

   Blue Sky Grocery and Grill (Press Enter.)
   555-9292 (Press Enter.)

The WordPad window looks like this:

4. Click the Save button. You haven't yet named the document, so WordPad displays the Save As dialog box (see page 34).

The Up One Level button

5. If Staff Party doesn't appear in the Look In box, click the Up One Level button or click the arrow to the right of the Look In box to locate the (C:) folder, and double-click Staff Party.

6. Double-click *Document* in the File Name edit box, and type *Caterers* as the file name. Then, with Rich Text Format (RTF) selected as the Save As Type setting, click Save.

Suppose you are using your handy list to call the caterers and get estimates. The first caterer quotes you a per-person price of $6.25 for a regular assortment of appetizers and $7.75 for a deluxe assortment. You want to know the respective costs for 72 people. This is a job for Calculator:

Using taskbar buttons

1. Click the Calculator button on the taskbar to bring the Calculator window to the foreground.

2. Click the buttons for 72, click *, click the buttons for 6.25, and click =. (You can press the numeric keypad keys if Numlock is turned on.) The display bar shows the total, 450.

3. Click the WordPad button on the taskbar to display its window. The Calculator window is once again obscured.

4. Click at the beginning of the blank line after the first caterer's telephone number to position the insertion point there, type *Regular: $450*, and press Enter.

Here's another way to switch between open programs:

1. Hold down the Alt key and, without releasing it, press the Tab key. A window appears in the middle of the screen in which icons represent the open programs. A box indicates which program Windows will switch to when you release the Alt key.

Using Alt+Tab

2. Still holding down the Alt key, press Tab again to move the box to the icon of the other program. Press Tab again and then release the Alt key. Windows displays the Calculator window.

3. Click the CE (for *clear entry*) button, click the buttons for 72, click *, click the buttons for 7.75, and then click =. The display bar shows the total, 558.

4. Switch back to WordPad using the Alt+Tab combination. (From now on, we'll designate key combinations this way.) With the insertion point at the beginning of the blank line after the regular cost, type *Deluxe: $558*, and press Enter.

Now suppose the second deli has quoted you a per-person price of $5.75 for a regular assortment of appetizers and $7.25 for a deluxe assortment. You have only a couple of programs open, so let's first arrange them so that you can see them both at the same time, and then let's enter the information for the second deli:

1. Right-click a blank area of the taskbar and choose Tile Windows Vertically from the shortcut menu to arrange the open windows side-by-side.

2. Click the Calculator window's title bar to activate it, click CE, click the buttons for 72, click *, click the buttons for 5.75, and then click =. The display bar shows the total, 414.

3. Click the Caterers window, click an insertion point at the beginning of the blank line after the second caterer's telephone number, type *Regular: $414*, and press Enter.

More about Calculator

Calculator is capable of performing much more complex functions than those we describe here, and it provides several buttons you can use to store calculations. To find out the exact function of a particular button, as well as its keyboard shortcut, right-click it and choose What's This? from the shortcut menu. To display a scientific calculator, choose Scientific from the View menu.

4. Repeat steps 2 and 3 with the deluxe $7.25 amount to calculate the second caterer's deluxe cost and enter it in the document. Your screen looks like this:

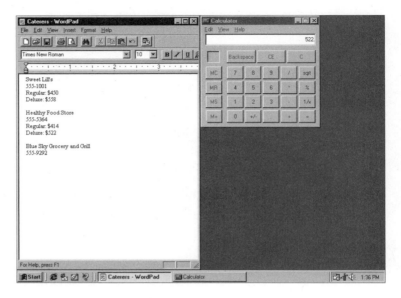

Sharing Information Among Programs

With Windows, it is easy to use the information from one program in another program. Need a logo for your letterhead? You can create one with a paint program, copy it to a storage area in memory called the *Clipboard*, and then paste it into a word-processing document. Because Windows allows you to run the paint program and the word-processing program simultaneously, moving from one program to the other is a simple matter of clicking the mouse button.

Let's experiment with transferring information using Word-Pad and Calculator. Follow these steps to complete the information for the third caterer:

1. Click the Calculator window, click CE, click the buttons for 72, click *, click the 6 button, and click =. The display bar shows the regular appetizer cost at $6 per person, 432.

2. Choose Copy from the Calculator's Edit menu to copy the value in the display bar to the Clipboard.

The Clipboard

The Clipboard is a temporary storage place in your computer's memory in which data cut or copied from all open Windows programs is stored. You can use it to transfer data within the same program or from one program to another. Each object you cut or copy overwrites the previous object. (See page 49 to watch this process in action.) Because the Clipboard is a temporary storage place, shutting down your computer erases any information you have stored there.

3. Click the Caterers window, click an insertion point at the beginning of the blank line after the third caterer's telephone number, and type *Regular:* followed by a space and *$*.

4. Choose Paste from WordPad's Edit menu to paste the total from the Calculator into the document. Then press Enter.

5. Repeat steps 1 through 4 to calculate the third caterer's deluxe cost at $7.50 per person and paste it into the document.

To give you more practice, we'll show you how to use Character Map, a Windows program you can use to insert special characters in your documents. We're going to add an entry for a fourth caterer called Mom's Kitchen Café to the list. Follow these steps:

1. With the Caterers window active and the insertion point at the beginning of the blank line below the third caterer, press Enter, and type *Mom's Kitchen Caf.*

2. Click the Start button, display the Programs, Accessories, and then System Tools submenus, and click Character Map to display this window:

Starting Character Map

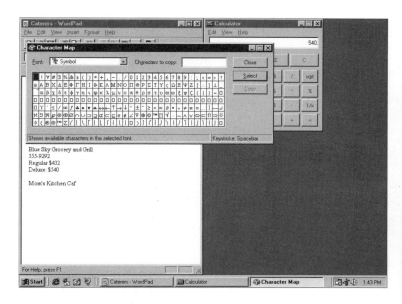

As you can see, the program displays all the characters available in the font specified in the Font box.

Entering characters with the keyboard

In the bottom right corner of the Character Map window is the shortcut for entering the selected character from the keyboard rather than by copying it from Character Map. For example, you can type the *é* character without switching to Character Map by holding down the Alt key and pressing 0, 2, 3, and 3 (0233) on your keyboard's numeric keypad. (You can't use the number keys across the top of your keyboard.)

3. Click the arrow at the right end of the Font box and select Times New Roman from the drop-down list. The characters in the grid below change to reflect those available in that font.

4. Check that the Characters To Copy box is empty (if it's not, double-click the existing entry and press the Delete key), click *é* in the last row, verify that it's the character you want, and click the Select button. The program enters *é* in the Characters To Copy box, and the window now looks like this:

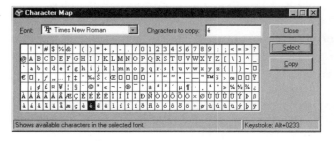

5. Click the Copy button to copy the character to the Clipboard, and then minimize the Character Map window.

The Paste button

6. With the Caterers document active, click the Paste button on the toolbar. The character you copied in the Character Map window appears at the insertion point.

The font size of *é* is 12 points, but the rest of the Caterers document is 10 points. To fix this problem, follow these steps:

1. Select *é* by dragging the mouse pointer over it so that it becomes highlighted. (If you have trouble selecting a single character with the mouse, point to the left of the line and click to select the entire line.)

More about fonts

Windows 98 comes with a set of fonts, and some programs add fonts to that set when you install them. When working with a program, you can see which fonts are available by clicking the arrow to the right of the Font box. When you are not working in a program, you can choose Settings and then Control Panel from the Start menu and then double-click the Fonts folder. To see a sample of a font, double-click the font's icon. To print the sample, click the Print button and then click OK. The sample includes a font description and examples in several sizes. Fonts are measured in terms of their height—the distance from the bottom of the descender characters in the font, such as *p*, to the top of the ascender characters, such as *h*. The unit of measure is called a *point* (abbreviated *pt*), and 1 point equals 1/72 inch. So if the setting in a program's Font Size box is 12, the size of the characters is about 1/6 inch.

2. Click the arrow at the right end of the Font Size box on the format bar to drop down a list of sizes, scroll up if necessary, and click 10.

Now let's complete the information for the fourth caterer:

1. Press the End key to move to the end of the current line and then press Enter.

2. Type *555-6198* as the telephone number and press Enter. Here are the results:

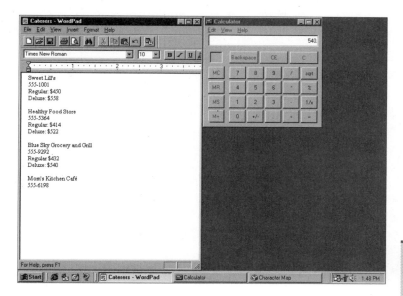

3. Click the Save button to save your work.

The last item you copied, *é*, is still on the Clipboard and stays there until it is replaced by the next item you cut or copy, or until you quit Windows. Let's sidetrack here to see the copied item on the Clipboard:

1. Click the Start button, display the Programs, Accessories, and then System Tools submenus, and click Clipboard Viewer. Windows starts the program, and it displays the copied text in its window.

2. Resize and move the Clipboard Viewer window so that your screen looks as shown on the next page.

Can't find Clipboard Viewer?

If Clipboard Viewer is not listed in your System Tools submenu, it has not been installed. To install Clipboard Viewer, choose Settings and then Control Panel from the Start menu. Double-click the Add/Remove Programs icon and then click the Windows Setup tab. Click System Tools in the Components list and then click the Details button. Click the check box to the left of Clipboard Viewer and then click OK to install the program. (You may need the Windows 98 CD-ROM to complete the installation.)

3. Calculate the cost of regular appetizers at $6.50 per person and copy and paste the result in the Caterers document, noticing that the copied item replaces the existing item in the Clipboard Viewer window.

4. Repeat step 3 to calculate the cost of deluxe appetizers at $8 per person and paste the result in the Caterers document.

5. Save the document.

Once you have created a document, you'll usually want to print it, so we'll discuss printing next.

Using Printers

Although computers were supposed to usher in the era of the paperless office, in our experience they have had the opposite effect. Even with the proliferation of electronic mail (see page 90) and computer-to-computer faxes, most people still need to be able to print their documents.

With Windows 98, you have three methods for printing: using a program's Print command, dragging a document to a printer icon, and using the Send To command. Whichever method you choose, the document is printed by the default printer. If you have only one printer attached to your computer, that

---

Clipboard Viewer

Unlike the Clipboard, Clipboard Viewer can store several items. To save something you have cut or copied to the Clipboard for use at a later time, first copy it. Then open Clipboard Viewer, which displays the copied text. Choose Save As from the File menu and enter a name and storage location for the item in the Save As dialog box. To access the item later, open the Clipboard Viewer and choose Open from the File menu. You can then copy the item and paste it in another program as usual.

printer is usually the default. If you have a choice of more than one printer, the default is probably the one you use most frequently. (See the tip on the next page for information about changing the default printer.) In this section, we assume you have installed one printer that is physically connected to your computer (a *local printer*), but the procedure for printing on a printer that is connected to another computer (a *network printer*) is basically the same.

← Local printers and network printers

Printing from a Program

You can print an open document from within a program by using the program's Print command. To demonstrate, let's print the Caterers document we've been working on in WordPad:

1. Choose Print from the File menu to display the dialog box shown here, which is typical of the Print dialog box used by most Windows 98 programs:

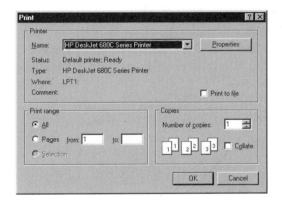

The Name box shows which printer is currently selected. The Status line tells you both that this printer is the default printer and that it is ready to receive your document. The Type line tells you the type of printer it is, and the Where line indicates the way the printer is connected to your computer. Finally, the Comment line contains any notes you have made about this printer. (See the tip on the next page.)

2. You want to print the entire document, so leave the Print Range option set to All. (With multipage documents, you can print only certain pages by clicking the Pages option and indicating the page numbers in the From and To boxes. Or you

Other printing options

The Print dialog box offers several printing options. For example, if you have more than one printer to choose from, you can use the Name drop-down list to select a printer other than the default one for a particular print job. The Status, Type, Where, and Comment lines then change to reflect the selected printer. You can get more details about the selected printer and change its settings by clicking the Properties button. (The Properties dialog box usually includes such settings as portrait or landscape orientation, paper size, and resolution.) Selecting the Print To File option turns the printing instructions into a file on disk instead of sending the instructions to the default location specified on the Where line. In addition to specifying the print range and the number of copies, you can tell some programs to collate multiple copies of documents that have more than one page.

can select part of a document and print just that part by clicking the Selection option.)

3. Next, in the Copies section, change the Number Of Copies setting to 2.

4. Click OK to print two copies of Caterers on the default printer.

Adding a Printer

The Add Printer Wizard

If you attach a new printer to your computer, you install it as a local printer using the Add Printer Wizard. To access the wizard, click the Start button and choose Settings and then Printers from the Start menu to open the Printers folder window. Double-click Add Printer to display the wizard's first dialog box, click Next to display the second dialog box, and click Next to tell the wizard you want to install a local printer. Scroll the Manufacturers list on the left side of the dialog box and select the manufacturer of your printer. The Printers list on the right side of the dialog box changes to reflect the printer models produced by the manufacturer you chose. Select the correct model from the Printers list and click Next. (If your printer is not listed, check the installation instructions that come with the printer. You will probably need to insert the driver disk that came with the printer and click the Have Disk button.) Select the port to which the printer is connected, and click Next. Leave the printer name as is or type a new name in the Printer Name edit box, click Yes to designate the new printer as the default printer, and click Next. To print a test page, click Yes and then click Finish. Windows may ask you to insert the Windows 98 CD-ROM so that it can copy the driver for the new printer to your hard disk. You then return to the Printers folder window, where the new printer is now listed.

If you are working on a network and your computer has a printer attached to it, you may need to share your local printer with other people who don't have printers of their own. To share your printer, first turn on sharing by choosing Settings and then Control Panel from the Start menu, double-clicking the Network icon, clicking File And Print Sharing, selecting the printer sharing option, and clicking OK twice. Close Con-

Changing your printer setup

If you need to make changes to your printer setup, such as renaming it, adding comments to it, changing the default, or deleting it, first display the Printers folder window by choosing Settings and then Printers from the Start menu. To rename a printer, right-click its icon, choose Rename from the object menu, type the new name, and press Enter. To add a comment for the printer, right-click its icon, choose Properties from the object menu, and in the Comment box on the General tab, type the comment, and then click OK. To switch the default printer, right-click the icon of the printer you want to be the default, and choose Set As Default from the shortcut menu. To delete a printer, right-click its icon, choose Delete from the object menu, and click Yes to confirm the deletion. If Windows asks if you want to remove the files used for the printer, click Yes or No, depending on whether you will use that printer again in the future.

trol Panel, open the Printers folder, right-click your printer's icon, and choose Properties from the shortcut menu. On the Sharing tab, click the Shared As option, type the name and any comment you want to appear in Network Neighborhood, and if necessary, type a password. Click OK to close the Properties dialog box, and then close the Printers folder.

To connect to a network printer (a printer connected to someone else's computer), double-click Add Printer in the Printers folder to start the Add Printer Wizard. Designate the printer as Network, click the Browse button to locate the printer, and specify whether the network printer should be the default. (If a password is required to access the printer, you will have to supply it during this installation process.) After the driver for the network printer is installed on your computer, you can print documents on the network printer as easily as you can on a local printer. If other documents are being printed, your document joins a queue and must wait its turn. You can see the queue by double-clicking the printer icon that appears near the right end of the Windows taskbar, next to the clock.

← Connecting to a network printer

Quitting Programs

When you finish working with a program, you will probably want to close it before moving on to some other task. Closing a program—also called *quitting*, *leaving*, or *exiting* a program—couldn't be easier. On page 28, we quit a couple of programs from the taskbar. Here's another method:

1. Click the Close button at the right end of the WordPad window's title bar. Because you have done some work since you last saved the document, WordPad displays a message box asking if you want to save the current version of Caterers.

2. Click Yes. The WordPad window closes and its button disappears from the taskbar.

3. Close the other programs the same way.

You can also quit a program by pressing Alt+F4; by pressing Alt, then F, then X; or by choosing Exit from the File menu.

Quitting a program that's crashed

To increase its reliability, Windows assigns each program its own area of memory to run in. That way, if a program crashes, it usually doesn't bring down the entire system. You can often close the misbehaving program and carry on working. To close the program, press Ctrl+Alt+Del (or Delete) to display the Close Program dialog box, then select the program, and click End Task. You will lose any unsaved work in the program, but your work in other programs should be unaffected. If this process doesn't work, other programs may have become unstable, and your best bet is to shut down and restart Windows. The moral: save your work regularly to prevent mishaps from becoming tragedies.

3

Managing Folders and Files

We track down and open existing documents using My Computer, Windows Explorer, Network Neighborhood, and the Find command. Then we show you how to get organized by creating folders and moving, copying, renaming, and deleting documents.

Use My Computer to
visually manage your
folders and documents

Use Windows Explorer to
organize your folders and
documents in list format

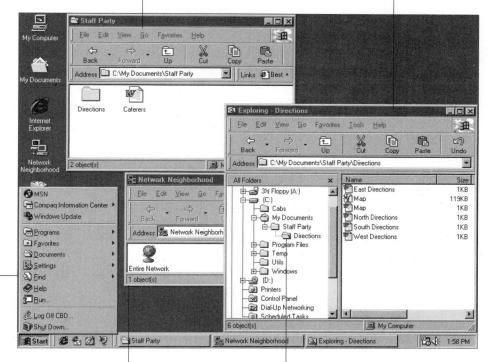

Locate folders and
documents with the
Find command

Use Network Neighborhood
to access folders and files
on networked computers

Create new folders to
organize your documents
for easy retrieval

For some people, organizing computer files is a difficult chore. They'll start a program, open a new document, save it with a name like *Letter*, and think that they'll be able to retrieve it without much trouble if they need it again. Because these people are busy, they often don't take the time to work out a file-naming system, and they may end up wasting a lot of time searching for a particular document. Is it *Letter*, or *Smith Letter*, or *June 12 Letter*? And is it stored in the Letters folder, or the Smith folder, or the June folder?

With Windows 98, you no longer have to trust your memory to organize and retrieve documents efficiently. First, you can use up to 255 characters, including spaces, in a file name. So you can use file names like *Letter Written On 6-12-98 To Smith Associates About The Hunter Project* to describe your documents. Second, Windows provides three organizational aids, My Computer, Windows Explorer, and Network Neighborhood, which you can use to shuffle your documents into folders in any way that makes sense to you.

In this chapter, we first discuss some organizational concepts. Then we show you how to find and open documents. We also give basic instructions for accessing resources on other computers if you are working on a network. Finally, we look at organizational strategies and techniques that make locating your documents as easy as possible.

Storage Basics

When you saved documents in Chapter 2, you saw that your computer storage space is divided into logical groups. For simplicity, you might want to think of this division as taking place on five levels:

The desktop

- **Level One.** The *desktop*, the by-now familiar opening screen of Windows, provides access to all the storage resources available to you while you are working. (The icon on the left is the Show Desktop button from the Quick Launch toolbar, which appears at the left end of the taskbar.)

Local and network storage

- **Level Two.** The desktop displays a My Computer icon representing your computer's storage, which we'll refer to as *local storage*. It also displays a Network Neighborhood icon representing the storage of any other computers available if you are connected to a network, which we'll refer to as *network storage*. Also at this level are the Recycle Bin, which holds objects you've deleted, and My Briefcase, which helps you coordinate the use of files on multiple computers. (For information about the Recycle Bin and My Briefcase, see pages 85 and 82.)

- **Level Three.** Your local storage is divided into chunks of space called *drives*, which are designated by unique, single letters. Most computers have one or two floppy drives, called *A* and *B*, and one hard drive, called *C*. If you have other drives, such as a CD-ROM drive, they are also assigned letters (*D*, *E*, and so on). If your computer is on a network, your network storage is divided into chunks of space on other computers, which are designated by the computers' names. The computers are further subdivided into drives designated by letters. Also at this level are four *system folders*: Printers, which stores a printer setup tool and printer information (see page 50); Control Panel, which stores tools for customizing the way you work with your computer; Dial-Up Networking, which you use with a modem to access computers that are not on your network (see page 96); and Scheduled Tasks, which stores information about tasks you want Windows 98 to perform regularly.

- **Level Four.** Divisions within drives are called *folders*. Some folders contain *subfolders* within them. (In this book, we use the term *folder* to mean any folder, designating folders within folders as *subfolders* only when the relationship is important.)

- **Level Five.** The lowest level is *files*, which are divided into two main categories: program files and data files. *Program files* contain the computer instructions that collectively constitute a software program, such as a word processor or a graphics program, and they are written by programmers. *Data files* are the documents you create while running a program, such as a letter written using a word processor, or a picture drawn with a graphics program.

For example, you might write a report called *2nd Qtr Sales* and store it in a folder called *1998*. This folder is a subfolder

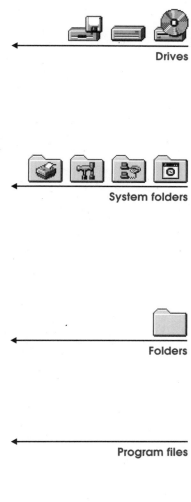

Drives

System folders

Folders

Program files

Data files

of a folder called *Reports*, which is in turn a subfolder of a folder called *My Documents*, which is stored on the C drive of your computer. Your computer is the local storage component of all the resources available from your desktop. If your computer's name is Sales1, the path of the document is *Sales1\C:\My Documents\Reports\1998\2nd Qtr Sales* (see the tip on page 36 for information about paths).

Bear in mind these levels of storage as we move on to explore ways of finding and organizing documents.

Opening Recently Used Files

When you want to open a document you worked on recently, you don't have to know where you stored it. For example, in Chapter 2, you created a document called *Directions*. Suppose you now want to change some of the instructions in the document. Follow these steps to open it and make the changes:

Opening a document from the Documents submenu

1. Click the Start button to open the Start menu and then point to Documents. Windows displays a submenu of the documents you have worked on recently, as shown here:

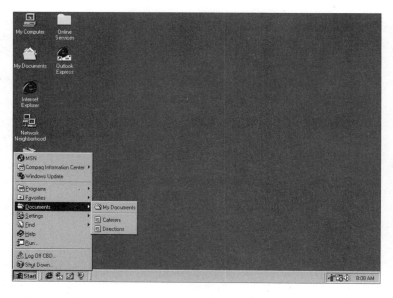

Clearing the Documents submenu

Sometimes you might want to start a Windows session with an empty Documents submenu to avoid the clutter of old documents you don't need. To clear the submenu, right-click a blank area of the taskbar and choose Properties from the taskbar's shortcut menu to display the Taskbar Properties dialog box, which has two tabs. Click the Start Menu Programs tab, click the Clear button in the Documents Menu section to remove the list of documents from the submenu, and then click OK to close the dialog box.

Programs can record up to 15 documents on this submenu. (Not all programs take advantage of this feature.) Once the submenu is full, older document names are deleted from the list as new ones are added.

2. Click Directions. Windows opens the document in its associated program so that you can begin editing.

Notice that you don't have to first start a program and then open the document. Windows knows which program is associated with the document and starts that program automatically. (If Microsoft Word is installed on your computer, Windows starts Word instead of WordPad because it assumes you want to use the more sophisticated word processor. Don't worry, our steps will work with whichever program Windows starts.)

Now let's change the memo and save it with a different name so that we will have a couple of documents to play with:

1. In the first instruction, change the word *North* to *South*. (Double-click *North* to select the word, and type *South*.)

2. In the second instruction, change the word *right* to *left*.

3. Choose Save As from the File menu to display the dialog box shown earlier on page 34, press the End key to move the insertion point to the end of the File Name edit box's entry, press the Spacebar, and type *From North*. Leave all the other settings as they are and click Save to save this new version of the document with a different name.

4. Click the Start button and point to Documents to display its submenu, which now includes Directions From North as well as the original Directions. (Notice that you don't have to close or minimize the document window in order to access the Start menu and do other types of work.)

5. Click anywhere away from the menu to close it.

6. Now click the Close button to close the Directions From North window and quit the program in preparation for the next section.

How does Windows know which program to start?

When you save a file, Windows adds an extension to the file name to identify the file type. File types are associated with programs. For example, if you double-click a file with an *xls* extension, Windows knows to open the file in Excel because the *xls* file type is associated with Excel. However, the associations might change as you install new programs. For example, the *rtf* extension is associated with WordPad unless you install Word, which takes over the association. To view or edit associations, choose Folder Options from the View menu of My Computer or Windows Explorer and display the File Types tab.

Finding Files

You've just seen how to open a document you have recently worked on. But what if you need to retrieve a document that you worked on a while ago? If you know in which folder and on which drive the file is stored, you can use My Computer, Windows Explorer, or Network Neighborhood, which all come with Windows, to locate and open it. If you're hazy about the document's name or location, you can use the Find command to track it down. We'll try finding a document in the next four sections. As you'll see, you can also use these techniques to find and start programs.

Using My Computer

My Computer is represented by an icon directly on the desktop because it is frequently used for basic file management. Using My Computer, you can navigate through your local storage by moving from window to window. The quickest way to become familiar with My Computer is to start using it, so follow these steps to find the Directions document, which is stored in the Staff Party folder on your C drive:

The My Computer icon

1. Double-click the My Computer icon to display a window. Notice that the window's button appears on the taskbar.

2. If the window is maximized, click the Restore button. Then size the window and choose Arrange Icons and By Drive Letter from the View menu, so that the My Computer window looks like this:

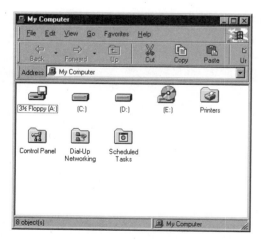

Finding My Computer

If you have several windows open on the desktop, or if a window is maximized, the My Computer icon may be hidden. To find it, click the Show Desktop button on the Quick Launch toolbar, which is located on the taskbar to the right of the Start button.

Don't worry if your window contains different icons than ours. Your icons represent the setup of your particular computer, and some of your icons may have different names.

We'll take a short side-track here to show you how to display information about the various drives in your computer. Follow these steps:

1. Right-click the (C:) icon and choose Properties from the shortcut menu to display the dialog box shown below. (If necessary, click the General tab.)

Displaying disk properties

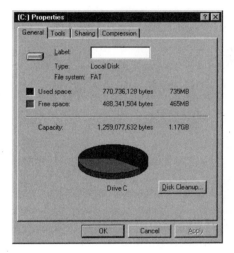

On the General tab, Windows reports the capacity and the amount of used and free space on drive C and displays this information visually as a pie chart.

2. Click OK to close the dialog box.

3. One at a time, right-click the other drive icons in the window, choose Properties, and check out their descriptions.

Now let's track down the Directions document:

1. Double-click the icon for your C drive to open a window that displays its contents.

2. Double-click the icon for the Staff Party folder to display its contents, which include the Directions document.

More about disk properties

You can display the Properties dialog box by selecting a drive in My Computer or Windows Explorer and clicking the Properties button on the toolbar. (You can also access this dialog box by selecting the drive and choosing Properties from the File menu.) This dialog box can be used to manage disks as well as check their capacity. For example, from the Tools tab you can run Scan-Disk, Backup or Disk Defragmenter; from the Sharing tab you can share the drive, and from the Compression tab you can initiate or modify disk compression. (We discuss sharing on page 68.)

Notice that clicking an icon opens a new window. Because the new window is active, it overlays the previous one. If you prefer, you can open just one window and have the window's contents change to display the contents of each new icon you click. (See the tip below for more information.)

Having located the Directions document, let's see how to open it:

Opening a document from My Computer

1. Double-click the Directions icon to both start the associated program and open the document.

2. Use the Save As command to save a copy of the document with the name *Directions From South.* (Before you click the Save button, be sure the Save As Type setting is still Rich Text Format.)

3. Click the Close button to close the document and quit the program, but leave the Staff Party folder window open.

Now let's change the way the contents of the active folder are displayed in its window. Follow these steps:

The Views button

1. Click the arrow to the right of the Views button on the toolbar to display a drop-down list of view options and then choose Details. (If you can't see the Views button, maximize the window.) Your view of the documents in the Staff Party folder changes to look like the one that is at the top of the facing page.

Using one window

To display only one My Computer window, choose Folder Options from the View menu to open the dialog box shown on page 9, click the Custom option and then click Settings. In the Browse Folders As Follows section, click Open Each Folder In The Same Window, click OK, and then click Close.

Other views

In addition to the Large Icons view and the Details view we show here, you can view the contents of a folder window as a set of small icons or as a list. To do this, simply select the corresponding option from the View button's drop-down list. Instead of using the View button on the toolbar, you can choose the same commands from the View menu.

The system folders

You can open the Printers, Control Panel, Dial-Up Networking, and Scheduled Tasks folders in My Computer and work with their tools. But you shouldn't think of these folders the same way you think of the folders you create. You can't move files in or out of the system folders, for example, and to avoid potential catastrophes, you shouldn't try.

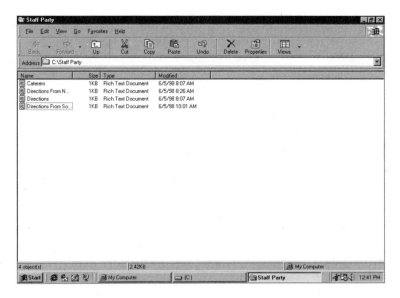

Now you can see each file's size and type, as well as the date it was last modified.

2. Click the Up button on the toolbar to move up one folder level. Notice that changing the view in one window does not affect the view in other windows.

3. Click the Staff Party button on the taskbar to switch to the Staff Party folder window.

4. Click the arrow to the right of the Views button again and choose List. The window now lists the files but not their details.

5. To open the Directions memo from this view, simply double-click the document name. Then close the document again.

6. Close all the folder windows by clicking their Close buttons.

We'll explore some of the other features and uses of My Computer later in this chapter.

Using Windows Explorer

Whereas My Computer displays the contents of a specific folder in its own window, Windows Explorer uses one window divided into two panes to show all your computer's storage. If you are familiar with File Manager, you'll recognize

The Up button

More My Computer techniques

To move up one folder level, press Backspace. To display a different folder in the active window, enter the folder's path in the Address bar. For example, type *C:\My Documents\Staff Party* and press Enter to display the Staff Party folder. To close multiple open folders, hold down Shift and click the Close button of the lowest-level folder window. For example, if the C, My Documents, Staff Party, and Directions windows are open, you can close them all by holding down Shift and clicking the Close button of the Directions window. However, using Shift+ Close in the Staff Party window closes C, My Documents, and Staff Party, but not Directions.

Windows Explorer, but at first you may be frustrated because it doesn't work in exactly the same way. Once you get used to Windows Explorer, however, you may abandon My Computer in favor of Explorer's power and efficiency. To see why, let's start the program now:

Starting Windows Explorer

1. Click the Start button, display the Programs submenu, and then click Windows Explorer to display the window shown here (maximize the window if necessary):

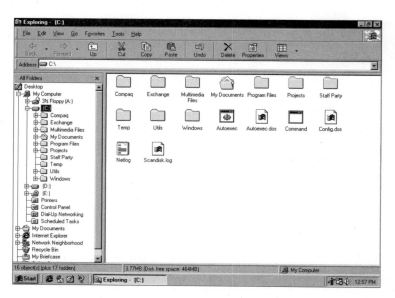

The right pane

Notice that the pane on the right looks similar to the Large Icons view of a folder window displayed in My Computer. (If your window shows a different view, click the arrow to the right of the Views button, and choose Large Icons from the drop-down list.)

The left pane

Windows Explorer's left pane displays a hierarchical diagram of all your available storage space arranged like this:

- **Level One.** At the top is the desktop.

- **Level Two.** One level to the right are My Computer, My Documents, Internet Explorer, Network Neighborhood, the Recycle Bin, My Briefcase, and Online Services.

- **Level Three.** One more level to the right are the drives and the system folders on your computer.

- **Level Four.** One level to the right on your C drive are all the folders stored on that drive.

The fifth level, files, is displayed only in the right pane.

You can expand and contract the diagram, displaying only the highest levels or zooming in for a closer look at folders and subfolders. Let's experiment in the left pane:

1. Double-click the (C:) icon. The folder icons on your C drive disappear from the left pane (collapse), and the minus symbol to the left of the (C:) icon becomes a plus symbol, indicating that the drive has hidden folders. (Instead of double-clicking icons, you can click the plus symbol to expand and click the minus symbol to contract the diagram in the left pane, without changing the view in the right pane.) Because drive C is still selected, its folders are displayed in the right pane even though they are no longer visible in the left pane, as shown here:

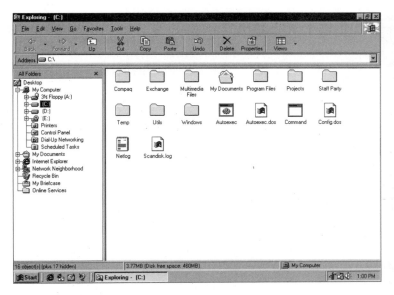

Displaying all files

When you open some folder windows, Windows may not display files that are critical to its own or a program's operation, because deleting or moving these files would create havoc. If you need to, you can display these files by choosing Folder Options from the View menu, clicking the View tab, selecting Show All Files under Hidden Files, and clicking OK. The change is implemented in both My Computer and Windows Explorer. For safety, you should work with the Do Not Show Hidden Or System Files option selected in the Folder Options dialog box, selecting Show All Files only on the rare occasions when you need to manipulate these important files.

2. Double-click the (C:) icon again. The folder icons reappear in the left pane (expand), and the plus symbol to the left of the (C:) icon reverts to a minus symbol, indicating that the folders it contains are not hidden.

Customizing My Computer and Windows Explorer

By default, Windows does not display some file types in the My Computer or Exploring windows. (Usually you don't want to touch these files.) To change this option, see the tip on page 65. To see more information in the My Computer or Exploring windows, you can customize the display of the toolbar and Address bar. To hide the labels on the toolbar, choose Toolbars and then Text Labels from the View menu to toggle off the command. If you don't use the Address bar, you can turn it off by choosing Toolbars and then Address Bar from the View menu. You can also move the Address bar to the right of the toolbar or menu bar by pointing to the word *Address* at the left end of the bar, holding down the left mouse button, and when the pointer changes to a four-headed arrow, dragging the Address bar up into the blank area at the right end of the toolbar or menu bar. Finally, you can customize the Exploring window by resizing its panes and columns. Simply point to the item's border and when the pointer changes to a double-headed arrow, drag in the desired direction. (Bear in mind that most of these customization techniques also work in other program windows such as the Recycle Bin and Outlook Express.)

3. Click the Windows folder icon once in the left pane to display the folder's contents in the right pane, but without expanding the diagram to display its contents in the left pane. (Notice that the folder's icon changes to an open folder.) This single-click technique is useful when you want to keep the "big picture" in view in the left pane as well as see the contents and details of a particular folder in the right pane.

You can also change the display by double-clicking icons in the right pane. Try this:

1. Double-click the Media folder in the right pane. Windows Explorer expands the diagram in the left pane to display the Windows folder's contents, opens the Media folder, and displays its contents in the right pane.

2. Click the Up button on the toolbar. Windows Explorer closes the Media folder in the diagram in the left pane, opens the Windows folder, and then displays the contents of that folder in the right pane. (Notice that clicking the Up button does not collapse the diagram in the left pane.)

3. Click the Up button again to display the contents of drive C.

Experiment with the Exploring window until you are familiar with the various techniques for displaying the contents of folders. Then rejoin us and follow these steps to open a document and start a program from Windows Explorer:

1. Display the contents of the Staff Party folder in the right pane.

2. Double-click the Directions icon to open the document in its associated program. Then close the document again.

3. Click the arrow to the right of the Views button and choose Details from the drop-down list.

4. Click the Windows folder icon in the left pane and then, using the vertical scroll bar, scroll all the way to the bottom of the right pane to check out its contents, as shown at the top of the facing page.

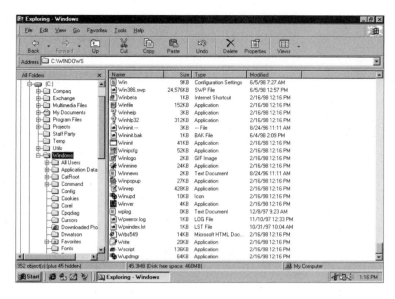

Notice the descriptions in the Type column and the various icons to the left of the file names.

5. Scroll the right pane upward until you see the Welcome application, and then double-click its icon to start Welcome, which displays the window you saw when you started Windows for the first time (see page 5).

Displaying the Welcome
window

6. Click the Show This Screen Each Time Windows 98 Starts check box in the bottom left corner to deselect this option. Then close the window.

7. End this brief tour of Windows Explorer by clicking the Close button to close the window.

You can start any program from Windows Explorer or from My Computer, so if a program's name does not appear on the Programs submenu of the Start menu, you can always use one of these handy helpers to track it down and start it.

Using Network Neighborhood

If you are working on a network, you will want to be able to find files on other networked computers, and other people will want to be able to find files on your computer. In this section, we discuss basic techniques for using Windows 98 to

Sorting

To quickly sort items in the Exploring window, click a column header in the right pane. For example, if you click the Modified header, the items are sorted with folders before files and the most recent items appearing first. Click the header again to reverse the sort order with files before folders and the oldest item appearing first.

Mapping network drives

To easily access folders from another networked computer, you can "map" the folder to a drive letter. Open Network Neighborhood, click the arrow at the right end of the Address box on the toolbar, and double-click the computer on which the shared folder is stored to display it in a window. Right-click the folder and then choose Map Network Drive from the shortcut menu. By default, Windows enters the next available letter in the Drive box. For example, if you have two floppy-disk drives (A and B), two hard drives (C and D), and a CD-ROM drive (E), Windows enters the letter F in the Drive box. Click the arrow at the right end of the Drive box to display a list of available drive letters, and select a letter for the shared folder. You can use any letter that isn't being used by another drive, disk, or shared folder. If you want Windows to attempt to reconnect to this folder each time you start the program, select the Reconnect At Logon option and then click OK. When the dialog box closes, the shared folder's contents are displayed in a new folder window. You can then work with the documents in the folder just as you would work with the documents on your own computer. The neat thing is that from now on the folder will appear as a drive in both My Computer and Windows Explorer so that you can access its contents with a couple of mouse clicks.

make the documents on your computer available to others and to locate other people's documents. If you are not working on a network, you can skip this section.

The way your system administrator has set up your network may limit the computers and files you can access and what you can do with them. If you see a message while following our examples telling you that you don't have this "right" or that "privilege," don't worry. The message just means your computer is not allowed to do what you just asked it to do.

Making documents available to a network takes three steps:

- **Set up file sharing.** First, your computer must be set up to allow file sharing. (This option is found in the File And Print Sharing dialog box, which you access by double-clicking the Network icon in the Control Panel window. Check with your network administrator before messing with any of the Network settings.)

- **Share the storage location.** Second, the drive or folder containing the documents must be *shared*.

- **Connect to the shared location.** Third, anyone who wants to use those documents must *connect to* that drive or folder.

We'll look at the second and third parts of this process.

Sharing Folders

Sharing a folder is easy, and because you can share folders rather than your entire hard disk, you can structure your folders so that only the information you want to share is accessible across the network. Moreover, you can assign passwords to shared folders to limit access to authorized people.

As a demonstration, suppose other people need to access the documents related to the staff party, which are stored on your computer. Here's how to make these documents available:

1. Using My Computer, display the contents of your C drive.

2. Right-click the folder you want to share (in this case, Staff Party) and choose Sharing from the shortcut menu to display this dialog box:

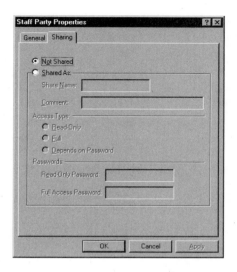

The Sharing command does not appear on the shortcut menu if your computer is not set up to allow file sharing.

3. Click the Shared As option. The name of the selected folder appears in the Share Name edit box. If you want to give this folder a different name for sharing purposes, you can enter a new name. We'll stick with the name Staff Party.

Naming shared resources

4. Click the Comment box and type any necessary identifying information. Other people will see this description in the Connect Network Drive dialog box when they are establishing connections to shared folders. As an example of a comment, type *July 4 Party, 1998*.

Adding comments

5. Now set access rights to the folder, as follows:

Setting access rights

- **Read-Only.** Select this option to allow other people to open files in the folder but not edit, delete, or move them.

- **Full.** Select this option to allow other people to edit, delete, and move files, as well as add new files to the folder.

- **Depends On Password.** Select this option to allow some people full access and others read-only access, depending on the password they enter.

  For this example, select Full. (If you select Depends On Password, you enter a password in the Full Access Password or

Read-Only Password edit box in the Passwords section of the dialog box. You then give the password only to the people you want to have access to the folder.)

6. You don't want to password-protect this folder, so click OK to complete the sharing procedure. Back in the folder window, Windows indicates that the Staff Party folder is shared by adding a hand to the folder icon, like this:

Now we'll move to another computer to show you how to access this shared folder across the network.

Connecting to Shared Folders

To use a document that is stored in a shared folder on another computer, you use Network Neighborhood to locate the folder and then, if you have the right to access the folder, you can open its documents by double-clicking them in the usual way. Here's how you would access the files in the Staff Party folder if they were stored on another computer:

The Network Neighborhood icon

1. Double-click Network Neighborhood on the desktop to open the window shown here (we've switched to Details view):

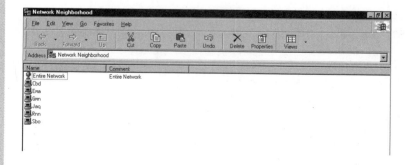

Using Net Watcher

If you choose Programs, Accessories, System Tools, and then Net Watcher from the Start menu, you can view a list of all the network computers currently connected to your computer and which resources they are using. (To use Net Watcher, you must have file and print sharing on.)

This window lists each of the computers in your workgroup and displays an icon for the Entire Network. (Clicking Entire Network shows you how your workgroup relates to others on the network and is useful when you need to share resources with other workgroups in large organizations.)

2. Double-click the computer on which the desired folder is stored. Because Staff Party is the only shared folder on this computer, the window now looks like this:

3. Double-click the shared folder. Windows opens the Staff Party folder and displays its documents.

If all access to a shared folder requires a password and you don't know the password, Windows will not connect you to the folder. If full access requires a password but read-only

Useful comments

If you want to display comments about the computers in the Network Neighborhood window, double-click the Network icon in the Control Panel window of each networked computer and type a description on the Identification tab. Using comments can help people on large networks locate computers and documents more efficiently.

Password lists

Windows associates a password list with your logon name and password. When you first connect to a shared resource, the resource's password is added to your password list. Then when you reconnect to that shared resource, Windows uses the password from the password list instead of requiring that you enter the password each time.

Suspending sharing

If you want to stop sharing your resources temporarily, you can do so by choosing Settings and then Control Panel from the Start menu, double-clicking the Network icon, clicking the File And Print Sharing button, and deselecting the sharing options. When you close the dialog box, restart Windows so that the new setting will take effect.

access does not, Windows will connect you to the folder and allow you to load and view files. However, you can't make changes to the documents, delete them, or move them. (You can make changes to a document and save it with a different name in a folder to which you do have access.)

To avoid having to traipse through Network Neighborhood every time you want to access this folder, you can simply "map" the folder to a drive letter. See the tip on page 68 for more information.

Stopping Sharing

If you no longer want to share a folder, you can discontinue sharing by following these steps:

1. In the interests of good working relationships, warn colleagues ahead of time that you are going to stop sharing, perhaps by sending a quick e-mail message.

2. In My Computer, display the folder or drive containing the shared folder, right-click the folder, and choose Sharing from the shortcut menu to display the dialog box shown on page 69.

3. Click the Not Shared option and then click OK.

As you have seen, Windows 98 makes using documents on networked computers as easy as using those on your own computer, hiding all the intricacies of the network so that you can focus on your work.

Using the Find Command

The fourth method of locating a document you want to open or a program you want to start is to use the Find command on the Start menu. Searches performed with this command can be pretty sophisticated, but the vast majority of searches are simple attempts to locate a document based on all or part of its name. We'll show you how to conduct this type of search and leave you to explore further on your own, using the Find window's Help menu if necessary. Let's get going:

1. With all windows closed, click the Start button, point to Find, and then choose Files Or Folders to display this window:

Finding other things

You can also use the Find command to search for other things. To search for a computer, click the Start button and choose Find and then Computer. Type the computer name in the Named edit box or use its drop-down list, and click Find Now. To search for information on the Internet, connect to your ISP and choose On The Internet from the Find submenu. Internet Explorer then opens and displays the Web page that you access when you click the Search button. If you choose the People command from the Find submenu, you can search through the address books on your computer to find information about the person whose name you enter. If you are connected to the Internet, you can also search an Internet White Pages directory, such as Four11, Bigfoot, Infospace, or WhoWhere to find someone. (Remember that you can also access these Find features via the Tools menu in Windows Explorer.)

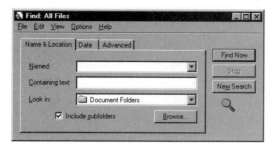

(You can also access the Find window from Windows Explorer by choosing Find and then Files Or Folders from the Tools menu.)

2. In the Named edit box, type *Directions*. Click the arrow to the right of the Look In edit box and select (C:) to search your hard drive. Then with the Include Subfolders option checked, click the Find Now button to start the search. Windows searches all the folders and subfolders on your C drive, and displays the results as shown here:

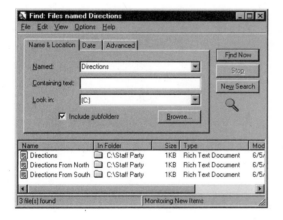

As you can see, Windows finds all the documents whose names include the word *Directions*. You can select a document and use the commands on the Find window's File menu to manipulate it in various ways, including printing, renaming, and opening it. (You can also open the document by double-clicking its icon.) If you are not sure which document is the one you want, you can take a peek at it by following the steps on the next page.

Specifying where to look

When Document Folders is the setting in the Look In box, Windows searches the My Documents folder. To search a specific folder, click the Browse button to display the Browse For Folder dialog box, then navigate to the folder, and click OK to return to the Find dialog box with the folder's path entered in the Look In box. (The path is added to the Look In drop-down list and is available for future searches.) To search all the subfolders of the specified drive or folder, be sure the Include Subfolders check box is checked. Otherwise, Windows searches only the top level of the specified drive or folder.

Quick viewing a document

1. Right-click the icon to the left of the Directions document's name and choose Quick View from the shortcut menu. (The command does not appear on the shortcut menu if the selected document can't be viewed.) You see a window like this one:

```
Directions - Quick View                              _ □ ×
File  View  Help

 ▣  A  A⁺  ▤
MEMO                                                    ▲

To: All Staff
From: Julia
Date: June 04, 1998
Subject: Directions to staff party


As promised, here are directions to Adventure
Works. See you all there on July 4!

1. Take I-5 North to Alderfield.
2. Take Exit 217 and turn right onto Route 24.
3. Follow the road up-hill and down-dale for 7 miles,
until you see the Alpine Ski Center on your left.
4. Turn right onto Park Road, and the entrance to
the park is immediately on the left by the totem
pole.
                                                        ▼
◄                                                      ►
To edit, click Open File for Editing on the File menu.
```

2. This is the document you want, so choose Open File For Editing from Quick View's File menu to open the document in its associated program.

3. Close the Directions window, and then close the Find window.

Organizing Folders and Files

As you have seen, using icons to perform common operations makes them less intimidating than having to remember commands. And the real strength of Windows becomes apparent when you use it to organize your folders and files by moving, copying, and deleting them.

Deciding on a System

Before you practice creating folders and moving documents, you might want to make a few decisions about what your folder and document structure should look like. When Windows 98 was installed on your computer, various folders were created on your hard drive to hold all the Windows files. When you install application programs, those programs also

---

More complex searches

In addition to searching for a document by name and location, you can search by modification date (when it was last saved) on the Date tab, and by file type and size on the Advanced tab. You can even search the actual text of your documents for a particular word or phrase. For example, you could search for a Word document that you saved between June 4 and June 14, 1998 and that contains the words *Adventure Works*. You can specify that Windows should find only files containing text with the exact capitalization you type, by choosing Case Sensitive from the Options menu. When you finish one search, you can start a new one by clicking the New Search button, and you can interrupt a search by clicking the Stop button. If you want to save the results of a search, first choose Save Results from the Options menu, and then choose Save Search from the File menu. The results are saved as a file with an icon on the desktop, so the next time you need to conduct that particular search, you can double-click the icon to retrieve the results, rather than having to search all over again.

create folders. Our concern here is not with these program folders. In fact, unless you really know what you're doing, it is best to leave program folders alone. Our concern is instead with the folders you will create to hold your own documents.

Because you can use long folder names and file names with Windows 98, you might think it would be easy to name documents so that they are readily identifiable. And there's no question that being able to use several words helps. Gone are the days when you had to convey the content of a document with a file name of no more than eight characters. Nevertheless, coming up with a few rules for naming files is a must. If you have ever wasted time trying to locate a document, you will probably find that spending a few minutes now deciding how to avoid such incidents in the future will more than repay you in increased efficiency. And a file-naming convention is a must if more than one person on your network uses the same set of documents.

However you decide to set up your folder structure, we strongly recommend that you store all the folders and documents you create in the My Documents folder. (Windows 98 stores this folder on the C drive by default.) Using My Documents as an all-purpose storage location greatly simplifies the backing up of your work, because you can back up the folder and all its subfolders in one operation. We also recommend that, to the extent possible, you use some unique document identifier at the beginning of each file name, especially if the document is likely to be used with a program that can handle only eight-character file names (see the adjacent tip).

Otherwise, there are no hard and fast rules for organizing documents, and the scheme you come up with will depend on your organization's requirements and the nature of your work. For example, if your documents are client-based, it makes sense to identify them by client. You might use the date as the document's unique identifier, followed by the client's name, followed by the type of document. Thus, a file name like *5-20 Smith Letter* might designate a letter written to Smith Associates on May 20, and the file name *6-14 Smith Invoice* might designate an invoice sent to the same client a few weeks later.

Short file names

Long file names work fine as long as you do all your work with programs designed to run under Windows 98 (or Windows 95), but if you are still using programs designed to run under MS-DOS, think carefully about the file names you assign in Windows programs. For example, suppose you create a Word document called *1998 Product Brochure* and you later need to open it in an MS-DOS program. When you look for the document while working in that program, you'll see the file name 1998PR~1.DOC. Windows converts the file name to eight characters, closing up the space, using a tilde (~) to indicate that it has truncated the name, and unhiding the three-character extension. If you have several documents with long file names that start with the same eight characters (*1998 Product List, 1998 Product Reviews, 1998 Product Proposals,* and so on), their short file names are distinguished only by the number added to each file name (1998PR~1.DOC, 1998PR~2.DOC, and so on), at which point it becomes difficult to know at a glance which document is which. So if you need to work with documents in both Windows 98 and MS-DOS programs, try to assign file names that work well in both environments. (You can see what the short file name will be by selecting the document in My Computer or Windows Explorer, clicking the Properties button on the toolbar, and checking the MS-DOS Name setting.)

The important thing is to come up with a simple scheme and to apply it consistently. You can then use Windows to manipulate the documents individually and in groups. For example, suppose you have accumulated so many documents in your client folders that you need to subdivide your client documents by type to make them more manageable. You can create a subfolder called *Invoices*, select all the documents in the client folder that have *Invoice* as part of their filenames, and drag all the invoice documents to the new folder. In the following sections, we'll demonstrate organizational tasks like this one by using My Computer and Windows Explorer.

Creating New Folders

You saw in Chapter 2 how to create a new folder while saving a document (see page 34). Now we're going to create another folder to organize the documents you've created so far:

1. Close all open windows, start My Computer by double-clicking its icon on the desktop, and display the contents of the Staff Party folder, which is on your C drive.

2. With the Staff Party folder window open, choose New and then Folder from the File menu to display a new folder icon within the Staff Party window.

3. With the new folder selected, type *Directions* to replace the highlighted text and then press Enter.

Keep it simple

In an eagerness to impose structure, some people go overboard, developing convoluted naming systems and subfolder mazes in which it is easy to get lost. The result is usually as bad as no system at all, because it is then less hassle to create file names on the fly and search a huge folder than it is to recall how the system works. Remember, to take advantage of the file-organization capabilities of Windows, keep your system simple.

4. Minimize the My Computer window and close any other open windows to reduce screen clutter.

5. Start Windows Explorer, this time by right-clicking the My Computer icon and choosing Explore from the shortcut menu. (The Explore command appears on many shortcut menus to make the Exploring window readily available.)

6. Double-click the (C:) icon to display its contents, which include a My Documents folder.

7. Minimize the Exploring window.

Specifying What You Want to Work With

Having created the new folder, you're ready to select the documents you want to move or copy into it. You've already seen how to click an icon to select it. Here, we'll show you a few other methods for selecting that work in both My Computer and Windows Explorer:

1. Click the Staff Party button on the taskbar.

2. Next, click the first document icon, hold down the Shift key, click the last document icon, and release Shift. The entire set of documents is now selected. In the status bar, the number of selected documents and their total size is displayed. You can see the size only if the window is maximized or is at least as wide as the one shown here:

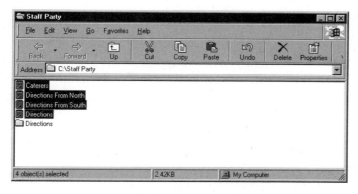

3. Hold down the Ctrl key, click the Directions document icon, and release Ctrl. That icon is no longer part of the selection.

4. Click the Directions folder icon. Now only that icon is selected.

5. Choose Invert Selection from the Edit menu to deselect the selected icon and select the other icons in the window. (This command is convenient when a folder contains many documents and you want to select all but a few of them.)

Switching selected and unselected documents

6. Click an empty area of the window to deselect everything.

If a My Computer folder window or the right pane of the Exploring window displays large icons, you can drag a selection rectangle around the icons of the files you want to work with.

Dragging a selection rectangle

Point close to, but not at, the first icon, hold down the left mouse button, and drag beyond the last icon. The rectangle expands as you drag, highlighting each icon it encloses. Release the button when everything you want is selected.

Moving and Copying Folders and Files

As a demonstration, we are going to move the Staff Party folder into the My Documents folder and then copy documents from the Staff Party folder to the new Directions subfolder. Follow these steps:

1. Click the Up button to display the contents of the C drive, and then close the Staff Party folder window.

2. Make sure you can see both the My Documents and Staff Party folders. (Size the window and switch to Large Icons view if necessary.)

3. Click the Staff Party folder icon to select it, hold down the *right* mouse button, and drag the dotted image of the selected icon over the My Documents icon. (The destination icon changes color when the pointer is in the right place.) When you release the mouse button, you see this shortcut menu:

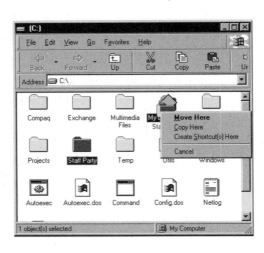

4. Choose Move Here to move the folder and its contents into the My Documents folder. The Staff Party icon disappears from the (C:) window.

Shift vs. Ctrl

When selecting objects in a folder window or Windows Explorer, holding down Shift while clicking extends the selection to all the objects up to and including the one you clicked last. For example, if the second object is selected, holding down Shift and clicking the fourth object extends the selection to include the second, third, and fourth objects. Holding down Ctrl while clicking adds only the clicked object to the selection. For example, if the second object is selected, holding down Ctrl and clicking the fourth object adds the fourth object, so that the second and fourth objects are selected but not the third. Holding down Ctrl while clicking a selected object removes that object from the selection without deselecting anything else.

5. To see if the folder and its documents have moved, double-click the My Documents folder to display its contents, like this:

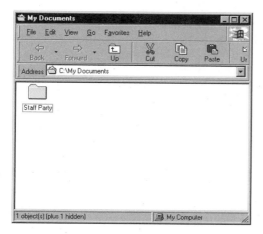

Next, we'll use Windows Explorer to move a document to the new Directions folder, and then we'll copy another document. The secret to efficient moving and copying in the Exploring window is to make sure the destination folder is visible before you select the folder or document you want to move or copy. Try this:

1. Click the Exploring button on the taskbar and double-click the My Documents icon in the left pane.

2. Double-click the Staff Party icon in the left pane and then select Directions From North in the right pane.

3. Using the *left* mouse button, drag the dotted image of the selected document over the Directions folder in the left pane. When you release the mouse button, the Directions From North icon disappears from the right pane.

4. Select Directions From South, hold down the Ctrl key, and using the *left* mouse button, drag the dotted image of the selected icon over the Directions folder. As you drag, a plus sign is displayed below the pointer to indicate that you are copying the document, not moving it. Release the mouse button and then release the Ctrl key. (If you release the Ctrl key first, Windows moves the document instead.) This time, the selected document's icon remains in the right pane.

Does Windows copy or move by default?

When you use the left mouse button to drag a folder or document to a new location on the same drive, Windows moves the object, unless you hold down the Ctrl key, in which case it copies the object. When you use the left mouse button to drag between drives, Windows copies the object, unless you hold down the Shift key, in which case it moves the object. If you find this logic confusing, use the right mouse button to drag so that you can choose the correct action from the shortcut menu.

Widening columns

5. Click the Directions icon in the left pane to display its contents in the right pane, and verify that the moved or copied documents are safely stored in their new folder, as shown below. (To widen the Name column so that you can see the entire name, double-click the border between the Name and Size column headers.)

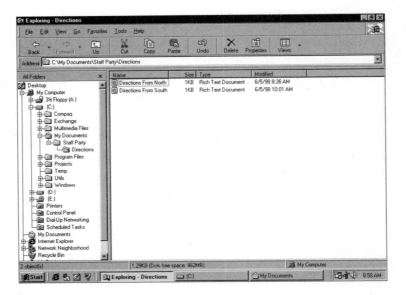

Follow these steps to copy a document within the same folder:

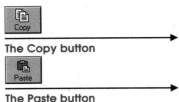

The Copy button

The Paste button

1. Click the Directions From North icon in the right pane to select it and click the Copy button on the toolbar. Windows puts a copy of the document on the Clipboard.

2. Click the Directions folder in the left pane and click the Paste button on the toolbar. Windows pastes a copy of the Clipboard's contents back into the Directions folder, naming the new document *Copy Of Directions From North*.

You can use the same technique to copy documents from one folder to another. This method also works in My Computer, but let's try another way:

1. Display the My Documents folder window by clicking its button on the taskbar, and then open the Staff Party folder window by double-clicking its icon.

2. Right-click the Directions document icon and choose Copy from the shortcut menu.

3. Right-click the Directions folder icon and choose Paste from the shortcut menu.

4. Double-click the Directions folder icon to see the results of the copy and paste procedure. As you can see here, you now have four documents in this folder:

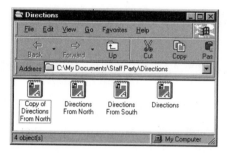

Copying Files to and from Floppy Disks

If you work on more than one computer, or if you share documents with colleagues but are not on a network, you need to use floppy disks to get documents from one computer to another. You might also want to copy documents to floppy disks as a way of backing up your work. The first step in copying a document to a floppy disk is to insert a formatted disk in the appropriate drive, so let's take a detour to discuss how to format floppy disks. To practice formatting, you'll need a floppy disk that is either new or that contains information you don't mind losing (formatting destroys any data already stored on the disk). Then follow these steps:

1. Close all open windows and double-click the My Computer icon on the desktop to display the My Computer window.

2. Insert a disk in the floppy drive and right-click the drive's icon in the My Computer window to display its shortcut menu.

3. Choose Format from the menu to display the dialog box as shown on the next page.

More about formatting

You can also format a floppy disk in Windows Explorer by right-clicking the floppy drive's icon and choosing Format. To assign a label to the disk, type it in the Label edit box. To format a disk quickly, select Quick (Erase) to erase the disk's file record without actually erasing the files themselves. To copy the files needed to start (boot) the computer, click one of the Copy System Files options.

4. Check that the value in the Capacity box is correct for the disk you are formatting. (You can select a different capacity from the drop-down list.)

5. Select Full as the Format Type option and then click Start. Windows formats the disk, displaying its progress in the bar at the bottom of the dialog box. When Windows finishes formatting the disk, it displays a Format Results box which displays the total disk space and the total disk space available. (These numbers will match unless there is something wrong with the disk.)

6. Click Close to close the message box and then close the Format dialog box.

Copying entire disks

To copy one disk to another disk, right-click the source drive's icon in My Computer or Windows Explorer and choose Copy Disk from the shortcut menu. Select the drive to copy from in the first box and the drive you want to copy to in the second box. (If you're using the same drive for both disks, select it in both boxes. Note that both disks must be the same type and format.) Click the Start button, and Windows walks you through the rest of the process.

Using Briefcase

If you frequently work on more than one computer—a desktop machine and a laptop, for example—you can use Briefcase to keep your documents in sync. To use Briefcase, first double-click the My Briefcase icon on the desktop of your main computer to open the program. Next, open either My Computer or Windows Explorer, drag the desired documents to the My Briefcase window, and close the window. Then, drag the My Briefcase icon to a floppy disk. Insert the disk in your other computer and work on the files in the My Briefcase folder. Then insert the disk in your main computer, double-click the My Briefcase icon, and click the Update All button on the toolbar. Windows then displays a dialog box showing which files need to be updated. Click Update to update the files on your main computer.

You are now ready to copy the Directions documents to the formatted disk. Follow these steps to try a couple of methods:

The My Documents icon

1. Double-click the My Documents icon on the desktop to open its folder window without having to go through My Computer.

2. Double-click Staff Party and then Directions to display the contents of the Directions folder.

3. Right-click a blank area of the taskbar and choose Tile Windows Horizontally so that you can see the four open windows.

4. Click the Directions From North icon in the Directions window and drag it over the 3½ Floppy (A) icon in the My Computer window.

5. Right-click the Directions From South icon and choose Send To and then 3½ Floppy (A) from the shortcut menu to copy the file to the disk in your floppy drive.

6. Verify that the documents have been copied successfully by clicking the arrow to the right of the Address box of the Staff Party folder window and selecting your floppy drive icon from the drop-down list of your computer's storage locations. Your screen now looks something like this:

Changing the contents of an open window

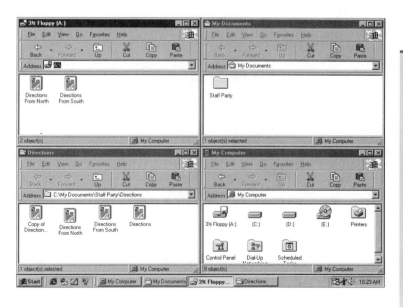

Many ways to the My Documents folder

In the steps above, you used the My Documents icon on the desktop. In the Exploring window, the My Documents folder icon appears in two places. In one place, it appears as a subfolder of the C drive, and in the other place, it appears at the desktop level. Rest assured that all of these icons lead to the same folder and are merely offered to give you several methods for accessing the My Documents folder.

7. Remove the disk and put it to one side for now. (You will use it again later in this book.)

You can copy files in the other direction (from a floppy disk to a folder on your hard drive) using this technique, and you can also copy in both directions using Windows Explorer.

Renaming Folders and Files

During the course of your work, you will sometimes want to change a file name. For example, suppose you want all the file names of the documents in the Directions folder to start with a unique word. Try these four renaming methods:

1. In the Directions folder window, right-click the Directions document icon and choose Rename from the shortcut menu. Then press the Home key to move to the beginning of the name, type *West* and a space, and press Enter.

2. Select the Copy Of Directions From North icon, choose Rename from the window's File menu, type *East Directions*, and press Enter.

3. Select the Directions From North icon, press the F2 key, type *North Directions*, and press Enter.

4. Finally, select the Directions From South icon, wait a second, then point to its name and click again to activate the name. Type *South Directions*, and press Enter. Here are the results:

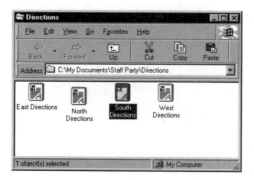

You can use any of these methods to rename folders, and the methods all work equally well in Windows Explorer.

Deleting and Undeleting Folders and Files

If you followed along with the previous examples, you now have two extraneous documents in the Staff Party folder. The potential for confusion is obvious, so let's throw out these duplicates using Windows Explorer:

1. Close all open windows and start Windows Explorer.

2. Display the contents of the Staff Party folder in the right pane, select the Directions document, and click the Delete button on the toolbar. Windows displays this message box:

The Delete button

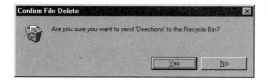

3. Click Yes to send the document to the Recycle Bin.

4. Next, right-click the Directions From South document and choose Delete from its shortcut menu.

5. Again, confirm the deletion when prompted.

   You can also make your selection and press the Delete key.

   These techniques can be used to delete a folder, its subfolders, and its documents with a couple of mouse clicks. A great shortcut, you might think. But it's wise to inspect the contents of the folder you are considering deleting and all its subfolders before carrying out this type of wholesale destruction.

   Fortunately, Windows provides a safeguard against the nightmare of inadvertently deleting vital documents. When you delete objects from your hard drive, Windows doesn't really erase them. As you have seen, it moves them to a folder called the Recycle Bin on your hard drive instead. Until you empty the bin, you can retrieve objects you have deleted by mistake. Try this:

1. Click the Undo button on the taskbar to restore Directions From South to the Staff Party folder.

Deleting without recycling

If you know you will never need a document that is stored on your hard drive, you can delete it permanently by holding down the Shift key while pressing the Delete key. This action is not reversible, so you should always think carefully before performing a deletion this way.

The full Recycle Bin

You could repeat this step to undelete Directions, but instead let's go rummaging in the Recycle Bin:

1. Minimize the Exploring window and take a look at the Recycle Bin icon on the desktop, which has changed to show that it has something in it.

2. Double-click the Recycle Bin icon to display its window, as shown below. (We have sized the window to make it smaller.)

3. Right-click Directions and then choose Restore from the shortcut menu.

4. Close the Recycle Bin window.

The empty Recycle Bin

5. Back on the desktop, notice that the Recycle Bin icon has changed to show that the bin is empty.

Now let's delete both documents again:

Deleting by dragging

1. Click the Exploring button on the taskbar, click its Restore button to shrink the window, and then move the window if necessary so that you can see the Recycle Bin icon on the left side of the desktop.

2. Select the Directions From South document, hold down the Shift key, and click Directions to add it to the selection.

3. Point to the selection and drag it over the Recycle Bin icon. After you release the mouse button, click Yes to confirm the deletion. Windows removes the documents from the Staff Party window.

If you are deleting files to free up drive space, your efforts won't yield results until you empty your Recycle Bin. Follow these steps to remove documents from the bin and completely erase them from your hard drive:

1. Double-click the Recycle Bin icon to open its window.

Emptying the Recycle Bin

2. Select Directions, press the Delete key, and then click Yes to confirm that you want to permanently remove the document.

3. Now choose Empty Recycle Bin from the File menu to erase the remaining contents of the bin, clicking Yes to confirm your command.

4. Close the Recycle Bin window.

5. Scroll the left pane of the Exploring window and click the Recycle Bin icon to view its contents. If the bin weren't already empty, you could also permanently delete items by right-clicking the Recycle Bin icon in Windows Explorer and choosing Empty Recycle Bin from the shortcut menu.

Displaying the Recycle Bin in Windows Explorer

6. Close all open windows.

If you are sure you won't need to restore any of the documents in the Recycle Bin, you can empty it without checking it by right-clicking its icon on the desktop and choosing Empty Recycle Bin from the shortcut menu. Click Yes to confirm your command.

By the way, Windows doesn't move objects deleted from floppy disks and the hard drives of other computers to the Recycle Bin; it actually deletes them. Always pause before clicking Yes in the Confirm File Delete message box when deleting files from anywhere but your hard drive, because this type of deletion is irreversible.

In this chapter, we have given you an overview of the tools Windows 98 provides to help you organize your documents so that you can quickly find them. Now it's up to you!

How big is the Recycle Bin?

To check the size of your computer's Recycle Bin, right-click its icon and choose Properties from the shortcut menu. By default, the bin occupies 10 percent of the hard drive on which it is stored, but you are able to adjust the size by moving the slider to the left (smaller) or right (bigger). If you have more than one hard drive, Windows maintains a bin on each one. Click the drive tab(s) to see how big the bin is on a particular drive. To set different bin sizes for each drive, you click the Configure Drives Independently option on the Global tab before you adjust the slider on each of the drive tabs.

E-Mailing with Windows 98

After a discussion of internal and Internet e-mail concepts, we show you how to use Outlook Express to send, reply to, and forward messages. You also learn how to use the Address Book, attach files, and organize messages.

Receive both internal and Internet e-mail in one Inbox

Easily identify a new message by its bold type and closed envelope icon

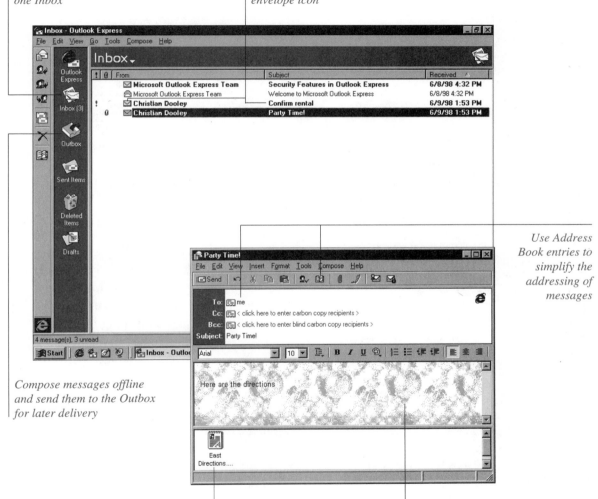

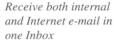

Use Address Book entries to simplify the addressing of messages

Compose messages offline and send them to the Outbox for later delivery

Send documents and programs by attaching them to messages

Dress up your messages with background stationery

People don't usually work in isolation. Whether you are using Windows 98 on a computer connected to a company or institutional network or on a stand-alone machine, you will probably use your computer to communicate with other people via electronic mail, or *e-mail*. In the first section of this chapter, we set the stage by exploring a few e-mail concepts. Then we look at how to send and receive e-mail using Outlook Express, which comes with Windows 98.

E-Mail Concepts

There's nothing difficult about the concept of e-mail. In the case of e-mail within an organization (*internal e-mail*), it's simply a way of sending messages that bypasses the traditional mail room. In the case of e-mail to the outside world (*Internet e-mail*), it bypasses the post office. The beauty of e-mail is that it doesn't use paper resources, it's fast, and it costs nothing (at least, nothing more than is already being spent on network resources and/or Internet access). Sometimes it is even better than using the phone because you can deal with important business right away rather than run the risk of playing telephone tag. Add to these advantages the ability to include files, programs, and other attachments with the messages you send, and the fact that you can send the same message to several people without any additional effort, and it's easy to understand why even people with abysmal letter-writing habits become staunch advocates of e-mail as a means of communication. Using e-mail, you can fire off a note to the person across the hall or to someone living on the other side of the world. You can share ideas with your organization's president or communicate with politicians and celebrities. (Of course, there's no guarantee that the recipients of your messages will actually read them, let alone respond to them!)

Like any other "good" thing, it's possible to have too much e-mail. Used wisely, e-mail can increase efficiency and reduce the amount of paper you use, but without a little restraint, e-mail can add unnecessarily to the burden of information overload. For example, if you get in the habit of copying messages to your entire department, everyone will feel obliged to spend time reading your messages whether or not they actually need

Inappropriate uses of e-mail

Just as there are inappropriate, and even illegal, uses of traditional mail services, there are also inappropriate uses of e-mail. Harassing or fraudulent e-mail is just as illegal as harassing or fraudulent regular mail. Mass e-mailing (junk e-mail, also called *spam*) and chain e-mailing are definitely frowned on by the Internet community. With regular junk mail, the receiver can decide at a glance whether to spend time and energy opening it. But with junk e-mail, the receiver is forced to spend time and resources (connect charges and hard drive space) before he or she can make that decision. Because of this intrusion, junk e-mails are sometimes punished vigilante-style. The messages are globally erased using programs called *cancelbots*, and the hard drives of their senders are swamped by replies that have huge-but-useless file attachments.

to. Bear in mind this potential for misuse as you begin integrating e-mail into your daily routine.

Internal vs. Internet E-Mail

Sometimes people confuse internal e-mail with Internet e-mail, and it's easy to understand why because in many ways, they are similar. However, having internal e-mail doesn't necessarily mean you have Internet e-mail, and vice versa. To be able to send e-mail to a colleague down the hall via internal e-mail, both your computer and your colleague's computer need to be connected to the company's network. To be able to send e-mail to a customer in another state via the Internet, both your computer and your customer's computer need to be able to access the Internet.

Let's briefly look at an example of internal e-mail. Suppose you want to tell a designer who is on vacation about a minor change in a product's specifications. You open a New Message window, enter the designer's e-mail address in the To box, enter a topic in the Subject box, type the message, and click the Send button on the toolbar. Information such as your e-mail address is added and then the message is sent from your computer to your company's *mail server*. The mail server holds the message in the designer's *mailbox* until she turns on her computer, at which time the e-mail program on her machine downloads the message to her hard drive. She can then read and reply to it at her convenience. The reply makes the same journey in reverse: from the designer's computer, it travels first to the company mail server, which holds the reply in your mailbox until your e-mail program downloads it to your hard drive.

How internal e-mail works

Now suppose you want to use Internet e-mail to drop a note to a customer thanking him for a recent order. Again, you compose your message and click the Send button, but this time the process involves a few additional steps. If you are working on a network, the message goes to your mail server as usual, and the mail server forwards it via the Internet to your customer's mail server so that he can download it at his convenience. If you are working on a stand-alone computer, your mail server

How Internet e-mail works

Internet Service Provider (ISP) →

is maintained by your Internet Service Provider (ISP), so you must connect to your ISP before your computer can send the message to the mail server. Your ISP's mail server then sends the message to your customer's mail server, whether that server is maintained by his company or by another ISP.

Obviously, for such a seemingly simple process to succeed as well as it does, some pretty complex things have to happen behind the scenes. But for the most part, none of that really concerns you, and we don't delve into the technology that makes each type of e-mail possible. Instead, our goal is to give you enough information to take advantage of these powerful communication tools.

E-Mail Addresses

E-mail addresses are like postal addresses, but instead of providing five or six items of information to send a letter to someone, you need to provide only one or two items to send an e-mail message.

Internal addresses →

Before an organization implements an e-mail system, the powers that be usually decide on a policy for assigning a unique e-mail address, or *alias*, to each mailbox. In smaller organizations, the aliases might consist of the first names of the mailbox users. Larger organizations might use first names plus first initial of last names, or some other scheme that is intuitive but avoids duplicates. So a typical internal e-mail address might be *chris* or *chrisd*.

Internet addresses →

A typical Internet e-mail address is more complicated. For example, the address for Christian Dooley might look something like this:

chrisd@fake.biz

If you had to say this e-mail address out loud, you'd say *chris dee at fake dot biz*.

The part of the address to the left of the @ sign is a *user name* that identifies the addressee, and the part to the right of the @ sign is a *domain name* that identifies the mail server where the addressee's mailbox is located. In our example, *chrisd* is the

Top-level domain names

Domain servers in the U.S. are organized into six top-level categories: *com* for companies, *edu* for educational institutions, *gov* for government agencies, *mil* for military agencies, *net* for network administration support, or *org* for other types of organizations.

user name and *fake.biz* is the domain name. (The last part of the domain name, identifies the type of domain; see the tip on the facing page. In this case, *biz* is fake.)

In the universe of e-mail, many users can have the name *chrisd* and many users can have mailboxes at *fake.biz*. But only one user named *chrisd* can have a mailbox at *fake.biz*. In other words, *chrisd@fake.biz* must be a unique address. If a user named Christine Doe wants a mailbox at *fake.biz* and *chrisd* already exists, she cannot choose *chrisd* as her user name. Either she must choose a name like *chrisdoe* so that her e-mail address is *chrisdoe@fake.biz*, or she must move her mailbox to a different mail server so that her e-mail address is something like *chrisd@false.biz*.

Every address is unique

Obviously, to send e-mail to someone, you must know the correct e-mail address. (See the adjacent tip for information about how to track down e-mail addresses.) If you send an e-mail message to a nonexistent address, it usually "bounces back," the equivalent of a return-to-sender stamp from the postal service, but if you send it to the wrong address, the results can range from negligible to disastrous. For example, suppose you send a message inviting Christine Doe to lunch but address it to *chrisd@fake.biz* instead of *chrisdoe@-fake.biz*. Christian might show up instead of Christine! More importantly, you might send a critical, time-sensitive message to the wrong address and never know why you didn't get a reply. The moral: double-check the address of the person you want to correspond with before you send a message on its way.

Setting Up Internet E-Mail

In order for people on a network to send and receive e-mail, the network administrator does all kinds of behind-the-scenes work to set up the mail server, establish accounts for each user, arrange for Internet access if applicable, and manage the whole system. If your network administrator has configured Outlook Express as your e-mail program, you can jump to page 97, where we tell you how to start Outlook Express. If you are using a different program, you can read along to get an idea of how things work.

Finding e-mail addresses

If you are working on a networked computer, your organization may provide an address book you can use to look up the e-mail addresses of your coworkers. If you need to locate an Internet e-mail address, you can use the Find People dialog box. Either choose Find and then People from the Start menu or choose Find People from the Outlook Express Edit menu. Next, select a directory service from the Look In drop-down list, enter the requested information, and click Find Now. If you are prompted to connect to your ISP, do so. After a few seconds, the results of the search are displayed in the list box at the bottom of the Find People dialog box.

The Connect To The Internet icon

If you are working on a stand-alone computer, Internet e-mail may not be set up, and you can't send or receive e-mail until you give Windows some information. Follow these steps:

1. Double-click the Connect To The Internet icon on your desktop to start the Internet Connection Wizard (or choose Programs, Internet Explorer, and then Connection Wizard from the Start menu). If necessary, identify your country, area code, and type of access and dialing. You then see this dialog box:

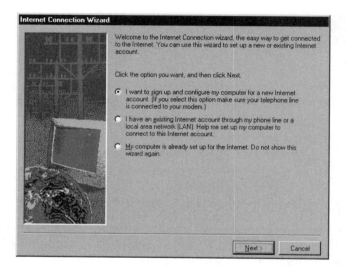

The Online Services folder

If you do not have an Internet Service Provider and would like to set one up, you may want to explore the Online Services folder. To open the folder, simply double-click its icon on the desktop to display links to some of the major ISPs, including America Online, AT&T World-Net, CompuServe, Prodigy, and the Microsoft Network. Double-clicking the icon of an online service starts a setup program that walks you through the steps of registering with the ISP. If you already have an account with one of these services, you can also tell Windows how to connect to it using this folder.

2. You now have three choices:

• If you do not yet have an ISP, select the first option, click Next, and follow the wizard's instructions.

• If your computer is already set up for the Internet, select the third option and click Next. The wizard closes, and the Connect To The Internet icon disappears from the desktop.

• If you have an account with an ISP but need to set up your Internet software to connect to your ISP, select the second option and click Next.

3. The wizard asks what type of Internet account you have. Select one of the two options and follow the wizard's instructions. As a demonstration, if you select the first option, you see this dialog box:

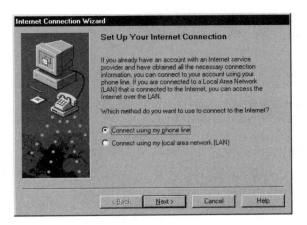

4. Click Next to use your phone line to connect to the Internet.

5. Enter the phone number of your ISP and click Next. Then enter your user (account) name and password and click Next.

6. Unless your ISP has told you to use advanced settings, click Next. Name this connection, click Next, and then click Next again to set up your Internet e-mail account.

7. Continue entering the requested information, clicking the Next button to move from one dialog box to the next. (If you don't have all the necessary information, ask your ISP to provide it. If you are unsure about any information, click the Help button to get assistance.) If you have never used e-mail on your computer before, you will need to enter the following:

- Your first and last name (for example, *Christian Dooley*).

- Your e-mail address (for example, *chrisd@fake.biz*).

- An Incoming Mail (POP3 or IMAP) Server name and an Outgoing Mail (SMTP) Server name (for example, *mail.fake.biz* for both).

- If your ISP does not use Secure Password Authentication, a logon name (probably the name you use when you connect to your ISP; for example, *chrisd*).

- Your password.

About passwords

A password is a security device designed to let authorized users into an account and keep unauthorized users out. Passwords can't serve this function unless they are secret. If you use a stand-alone computer to exchange personal e-mail with friends and family, the secrecy of your password may be a low priority. Otherwise, you will want to ensure that your password is complicated enough that it is hard to guess (combinations that include uppercase and lowercase letters and numbers are best) but not so complicated that it is hard to remember without writing it down. You should change your password regularly. (Your organization may alert you when it is time for a change.)

- A friendly name that Outlook Express will use for your mail settings (for example, *My Connection*).

You will also be given the opportunity to set up an Internet news account and an Internet directory service. Click No to skip this setup; you can always run the Internet Connection Wizard later to set up these options.

8. In the last dialog box, click Finish to save your mail settings.

Now let's check that everything is working properly:

The Dial-Up Networking icon

1. Double-click My Computer and then double-click the Dial-Up Networking folder icon to open this window:

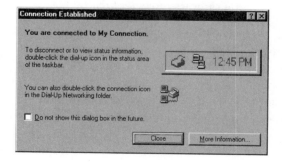

Testing the connection

2. If you have an external modem, make sure your modem is connected to your computer and turned on. Then double-click the icon for your connection to test it. (If necessary enter your password and click Connect.) When the connection is made, a modem icon appears to the left of the clock on the taskbar, and you see this window:

Disconnecting

3. Click Close, and then right-click the modem icon and choose Disconnect from the shortcut menu.

4. Close all open windows.

If you have any difficulty making the connection, contact your ISP for trouble-shooting assistance.

Starting Outlook Express for the First Time

Now that you all have your e-mail connections up and working, let's start Outlook Express and take a closer look at the program:

The Outlook Express icon

1. Either double-click the Outlook Express icon on the desktop or click the Launch Outlook Express button on the Quick Launch toolbar.

2. If you see this dialog box:

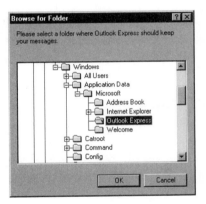

click OK. (Outlook Express won't show this dialog box again, now that it knows which folder to use.)

3. If Outlook Express displays this dialog box:

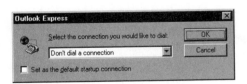

click OK to work with e-mail without connecting to your ISP, which is called *working offline*. (If you are using Internet e-mail on a stand-alone computer, you'll see this dialog box each time you start Outlook Express.)

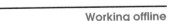

Working offline

4. Maximize the Outlook Express window, which looks like this:

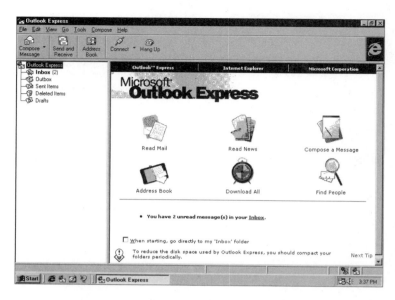

As you can see, the Outlook Express window is divided into two panes. The left pane displays a hierarchical diagram of the predefined Outlook Express folders. The right pane displays icons for the tasks you might want to perform, information about e-mail, and a tip for using the program. Across the top of the right pane are buttons you can click to go directly to three Web sites (provided, of course, that you are connected to the Internet).

5. Because you will usually want to go directly to your Inbox to view any new messages, click the When Starting check box and then click Read Mail.

Importing existing address books and messages

6. If you have previously used an e-mail program on your computer, the Outlook Express Import Wizard may appear to help you import your previous address books and messages into Outlook Express. Follow the wizard's instructions or click Cancel to close the wizard. (You can import them later by choosing Import from the File menu.)

7. If Outlook Express asks whether you want to use it as your default mail client, click Yes.

When the setup work is complete, you see an Inbox folder like the one shown here:

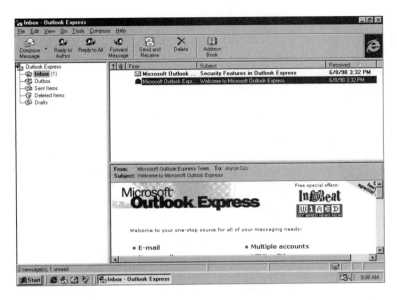

Outlook Express handles all e-mail messages through the Inbox window that is now on your screen, whether the messages were sent by a colleague down the hall or sent by a client on the opposite side of the world. In the left pane of the window, the Inbox folder is selected in the folder list. The selected folder's contents are summarized as a list of message headers in the top right pane, and the message whose header is selected in that pane is automatically previewed in the bottom right pane.

Customizing the Outlook Express Window

The default layout of the Outlook Express window may suit your needs as long as you have only a few messages in your Inbox folder. But after a while, you may find yourself wishing that you had more space to view your message header list. Let's take a look now at some of the ways you can customize the window:

1. Choose Layout from the View menu to display the dialog box shown on the next page.

Microsoft Outlook

Outlook Express is a stripped down version of Microsoft Outlook. In addition to e-mail, the full-blown program includes calendar and scheduling capabilities, a contacts manager, and a to-do list, as well as a journal for checking past activities and a handy notes feature. For more information, you might want to check out *Quick Course in Microsoft Outlook 98.*

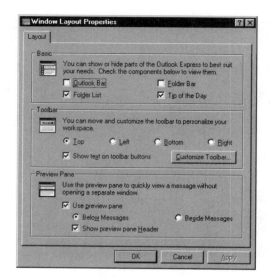

Moving dialog boxes ──────▶ 2. Move the dialog box to the right by dragging its title bar.

Displaying the Outlook bar ──────▶ 3. In the Basic section, select Outlook Bar and Folder Bar, dese-
and folder bar   lect Folder List and Tip Of The Day, and click Apply.

4. In the Toolbar section, select Left, deselect Show Text On
   Toolbar Buttons, and click Apply.

5. In the Preview Pane section, deselect Use Preview Pane and
   click OK. Here are the results:

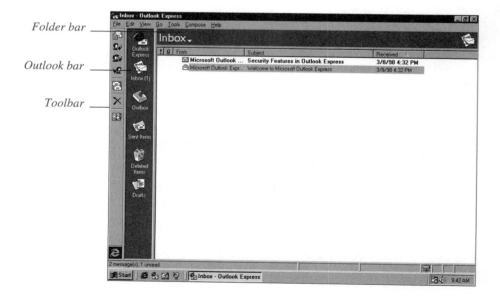

To see how to move around Outlook Express in this view,
follow these steps:

1. Click the Outlook Express icon at the top of the Outlook bar.
   The contents of the right pane change to display the options
   shown earlier on page 98, and the folder bar now indicates
   that you are looking at the Outlook Express folder.

Moving around

2. Click the arrow to the right of Outlook Express on the folder
   bar to drop-down the folder list, like this:

Displaying the folder list

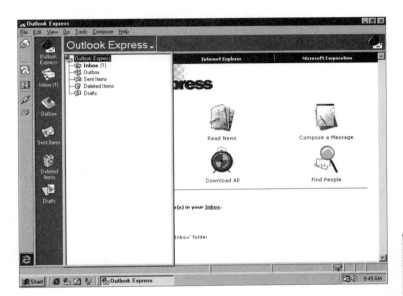

3. Click Inbox to redisplay the message header list.

   After you have worked your way through this chapter, you
   might want to experiment with various layouts to find the one
   that suits the way you work. But for now, let's move on to see
   how to send and receive messages.

Sending Messages

We'll look at the sending side of the equation first. For this example, suppose you are arranging the facilities for the staff
party and you want to remind yourself to confirm the rental
of Adventure Works first thing tomorrow morning. Follow
the steps on the next page to compose your first message.

E-mail etiquette

Your organization may have its
own *dos* and *don't*s, especially for
communications with customers,
but some general rules apply
when sending any e-mail message. Don't compose messages
in all lowercase or all uppercase
letters. The former is hard to read,
and the latter is considered rude.
(Sending rude messages is called
flaming.) To add flavor (tone) to
your messages, you may want to
use *emoticons* (sometimes called
smileys), which are combinations
of characters that look like faces
when viewed sideways. But be
careful: this practice can be tire-
some when overused.

1. Choose Work Offline from the File menu so that Outlook Express won't connect to your ISP until you tell it to.

The Compose Message button

2. Click the Compose Message button on the toolbar to open this New Message window:

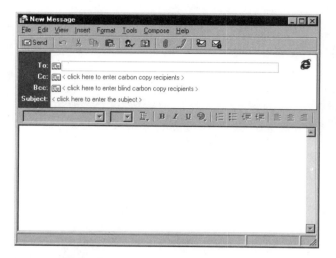

Keep the reader in mind

Some people receive so many messages that they need to be able to distinguish at a glance which they should read immediately and which they can read later. A Subject line like *A New Idea* says nothing about the content; *New slogan for Glacier Series* is much better. If the message is time-sensitive, start the Subject line with the word *Urgent*. If the message does not require any action on the part of the recipient, start the line with *FYI* (for your information). As for the message itself, avoid long paragraphs, which are hard to read on the screen. Also avoid long messages, limiting them, if possible, to one screenful of information so that the recipient can see the entire message at once.

3. In the To box, type your e-mail address and then press Tab to move to the Cc box. (To send a message to someone else, you type his or her e-mail address in the To box. To send a message to several people, you type their addresses one after the other, separated by a comma or a semicolon and a space.)

4. To send a courtesy copy of the message, you can enter the address of the recipient in the Cc box. For this message, leave the Cc box blank by pressing Tab.

5. To send a blind courtesy copy of the message (so only that recipient knows she has been sent a copy), you can enter the address of the recipient in the Bcc box. For this message, leave the Bcc box blank by pressing Tab.

6. In the Subject box, type *Confirm rental* and press Tab. (See the adjacent tip for pointers about efficient subject lines.)

7. Next, type the following in the message area:

Check on Adventure Works rental (555-0100). Be sure to tell them the caterers will be there at 10:00 AM to set up.

8. Choose Set Priority and then High from the Tools menu to designate this message as important. The message window now looks like this:

Flagging important messages

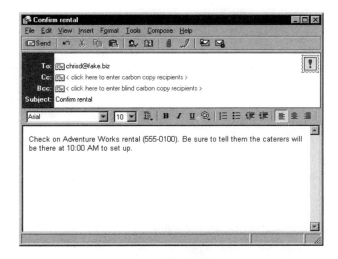

If you want, you can use the buttons on the Formatting toolbar above the message area to format the message.

The Send button

9. Send the message by clicking the Send button. If you are connected to a network or your ISP, clicking Send instantly sends the message to your mail server. If you are working offline, clicking Send transfers the message to your Outbox.

10. If the program displays a message telling you that you can send the message later by choosing the Send And Receive command, click the Don't Show option and then click OK to close both the message box and the New Message window.

If you are working offline, the Outbox icon on the Outlook bar indicates that you have one message waiting to be sent.

Shortcuts for Addressing Messages

After a while, you'll probably find yourself e-mailing a few people frequently. You can store their addresses in the Address Book so that you don't have to type them every time. Follow these steps to add an address to the Address Book:

1. Click the Address Book button on the toolbar to display the window shown on the next page.

The Address Book button

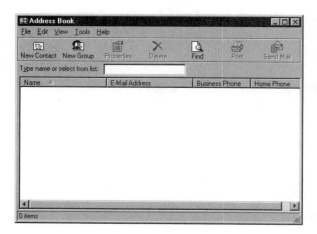

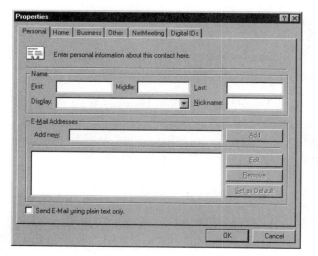

The New Contact button

2. Next, click the New Contact button on the toolbar to see this dialog box:

This dialog box provides a template for adding Internet addresses to your Address Book. If you are working on a network, your Properties dialog box may look slightly different, and in the following steps, you should substitute the name and alias of one of your colleagues for the President's.

3. In the Name section, type *Mr.* for the first name and *President* for the last name. Type *pres* (or any short, memorable word that strikes your fancy) in the Nickname box. In the Add New box of the E-Mail Addresses section, type *president@white-house.gov* and then click the Add button next to it.

Using groups

If you frequently send messages to the same set of people, you can create a group in the Address Book. Click the New Group button on the Address Book's toolbar and assign the group a name. Then either click New Contact to create a listing for someone new or click Select Members to add an existing address, and click OK twice. Enter the name of the group in the To box of the New Message window and press Tab to have Outlook Express enter the e-mail addresses of everyone in the group.

4. Enter any pertinent information you want to store on the other tabs of the dialog box, and then click OK to add this contact to the Address Book.

5. Click the New Contact button on the toolbar and repeat steps 3 and 4 to add your own name and e-mail address to the Address Book with the nickname *me*.

Now let's try sending another message, this time using the Address Book to see how it speeds up the addressing process:

1. With the Address Book window open, right-click *Mr. President* (or your colleague's name) and choose Send Mail from the shortcut menu. Outlook Express opens the New Message window with the correct e-mail address already in the To box.

◄ **Starting a new message from the Address Book**

2. Fill in the Subject box, type a message, and then click the Send button to send the message. (When you send a message to the President, you usually receive an automated acknowledgment from the White House, or you might even be chosen to get a response from a member of the President's staff.)

3. Finally, close the Address Book window. (If you are working offline, notice that the Outbox folder now contains two messages waiting for transmission.)

Attaching Items to Messages

With Outlook Express, you can attach several types of items to a message. In this section, we'll look at a couple of them.

Attaching Stationery

On special occasions, you might want to jazz up the appearance of a message by adding sets of predefined formatting called *stationery* (Bear in mind that not all e-mail users can view this Stationery.) Try this:

1. Click the Compose Message button, type *me* in the To box to insert your own address from the Address Book, press Tab three times, type *Party Time!* in the Subject box, and press Tab again.

2. Choose Apply Stationery and then Balloon Party Invitation from the Format menu. The background of the message area

Other Address Book options

You can organize your Address Book in a number of ways. To sort the information by first or last name, e-mail address, or phone number, simply click the respective column header. Clicking the header again will reverse the sort order (ascending vs. descending). To view only mailing groups, choose Groups List from the View menu and select the group to display its members. To erase a contact or group, select the entry and click the Delete button. If you want to convert a group member to an individual entry, double-click the group name, select the contact name from the Members list, and click Remove. You can print the Address Book information by selecting the relevant entries, clicking the Print button, and choosing a print style: Memo (all data), Business Card, or Phone List.

is now filled with a balloon pattern, over which you can type a message to yourself. (Don't click Send yet.)

Attaching Files

You won't need to attach stationery to messages very often, but you might need to attach files. As an example, let's attach one of the Directions memos to a message. Follow these steps:

1. In the open Party Time window, type *Here are the directions* and press Enter.

The Insert File button ────────►

2. Click the Insert File button to display this dialog box:

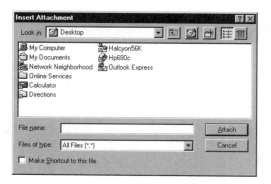

Attaching a signature

To create a signature that will appear at the bottom of your messages, such as your name, title, company, and phone number, first choose Stationery from the Tools menu, click the Signature button in the bottom section, and type the text of the signature in the edit box. (We recommend you keep it short and avoid being cute.) Click the Add This Signature To All Outgoing Messages check box if desired, and click OK. You can also add the signature to select messages by clicking the Insert Signature button on the New Message window's toolbar.

3. Double-click My Documents, then Staff Party, Directions, and East Directions. Outlook Express inserts an icon for the file in a separate pane of the Party Time window, like this:

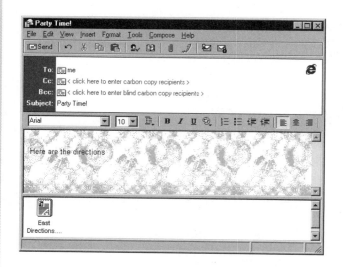

(If Outlook Express cannot locate the file, type the path *C:\My Documents\Staff Party\Directions\East Directions* in the File Name edit box, and click Attach.)

4. Click Send to move the message to the Outbox.

If you are working on a network, you can send a shortcut to the file instead of the file itself. Just click the Make Shortcut To This File check box at the bottom of the Insert Attachment dialog box before specifying the name of the file.

Attaching a shortcut

Sending Messages Stored in the Outbox

If you are working offline, you now have several messages stored in the Outbox, waiting for you to connect to the Internet so that Outlook Express can send them on their way. Here's how to send the messages:

1. Click the Outbox icon that is on the Outlook bar to see the messages.

The Outbox icon

2. Click the Send And Receive button on the toolbar. Outlook Express displays this dialog box:

The Send And Receive button

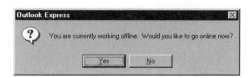

3. Click Yes. Outlook Express initiates the connection to your ISP, sends the messages, and checks for any new incoming messages. (You may need to enter your password.)

4. If necessary, disconnect from your ISP by choosing Hang Up from the File menu.

Retrieving and Handling Messages

If you are working on a network, your mail server probably routes messages automatically from your mailbox to your computer. (Usually, you will want to keep Outlook Express open while you work so that you can receive new messages right away.) If you are working on a stand-alone computer, you can retrieve messages that are waiting in your mailbox on

Attaching a Web page

If you want to send a hyperlink to a Web page with a message, first make sure Rich Text (HTML) is chosen on the New Message window's Format menu. In the body of the message, you can simply type a Web site's URL to create an active link to that site. Or you can select the text that will serve as the link, choose Hyperlink from the Insert menu, select the resource type, enter the path to the linked site, and click OK. Then simply send the message the way you usually do.

your mail server by clicking the Send And Receive button on the toolbar. (As you've seen, clicking the Send And Receive button also sends any messages stored in the Outbox.)

If Outlook Express is set up to retrieve messages according to a schedule (see the tip below), the program notifies you when you receive a new message by displaying an envelope icon at the right end of the taskbar and playing a sound. You can also manually retrieve messages like this:

New message alert

The Inbox icon

1. Click the Inbox icon on the Outlook bar.

2. If you don't see at least two new messages in your Inbox, click the Send And Receive button on the toolbar. (In addition to messages from the Microsoft Outlook Express Team and the two messages you sent to yourself, you might see a response from the White House.)

Sizing message header columns

3. Drag the borders of the column headings to adjust their widths so that you can see all their contents, like this:

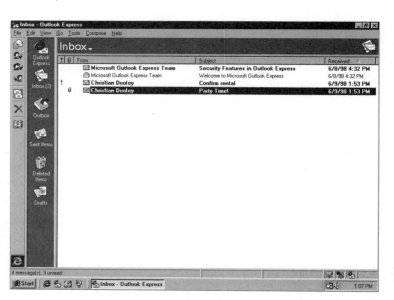

Scheduling mail delivery

If you are connected to your ISP and running Outlook Express, by default the program checks the server every 30 minutes for new messages. You can change this schedule by choosing Options from the Outlook Express Tools menu and adjusting the Check For New Messages Every setting.

Let's take a closer look at the message headers in the Inbox window. The headers include the sender's name, the subject, and the date and time you received the message. When you have not yet displayed a message, an unopened envelope is shown next to the sender's name, and the message header is displayed in bold. An exclamation mark in the first column indicates that the message is urgent, and a paperclip in the second column indicates that the message has an attachment.

Message symbols

Here's how to read a message:

1. Double-click the Party Time message. Outlook Express displays the message in its own window and changes the message header's unopened envelope to an opened one.

Displaying messages

2. Double-click the attachment in the bottom pane. Outlook Express displays a virus warning and asks what to do.

Accessing an attachment

3. Click OK to save the attachment as a file, and when Outlook Express displays the Save Attachment As dialog box, navigate to the My Documents folder and click Save. (If the file had been sent to you by a colleague, you could then scan it for viruses and read it at your leisure.)

Replying to Messages

Suppose the message now on your screen is from a colleague and requires a response. Follow these steps to send a reply:

1. With the Party Time message displayed in its window, click the Reply To Author button on the toolbar to open a window like this one:

The Reply To Author Button

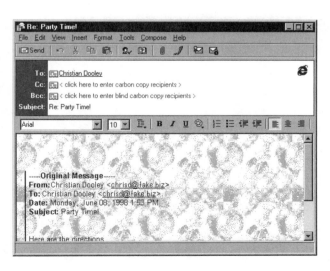

Viruses

You can't "catch" a virus by just looking at a file, but activating a file infected with a virus can wreak havoc. When you receive a file as an attachment, you should always store it in a folder and scan the folder for viruses before you do anything with the file. Although viruses usually do their damage via program files, new breeds of viruses attack word-processor and spreadsheet files. So get in the habit of scanning *all* attachments with a virus program.

The Reply To All button

Notice that the To and Subject boxes are already filled in. (Clicking the Reply To All button displays a similar window, except that the To box contains not only the address of the original sender but also those of all recipients of copies.) Notice also that the original message appears at the bottom of the message area, preceded by a vertical line. Outlook Express has inserted this text because the Include Message In Reply option is selected by default on the Send tab of the dialog box displayed when you choose Options from the Outlook Express Tools menu.

2. Type *Thanks. See you there!* and click the Send button. Outlook Express sends the reply on its way if you are connected to your mail server, or puts it in the Outbox if you are working offline.

3. If necessary, click the Send And Receive button and check out the reply when it arrives.

Forwarding Messages

If you receive a message that you think will be of interest to a colleague, you can forward the message with a few mouse clicks. Here's how:

The Forward Message button

1. Click the *Confirm rental* header and then click the Forward Message button on the toolbar to display this window:

Editing the text of original messages

To display only part of an original message or delete all of the header text in your reply, simply select and delete the text as you would in any other program. If you don't want to display the original message in any of your replies, choose Options from the Tools menu, click the Send tab, click the Include Message In Reply box to deselect it, and then click OK.

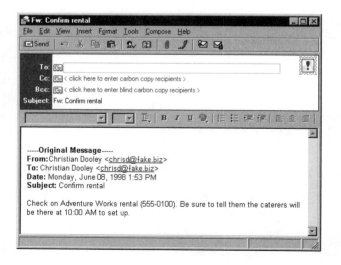

2. For demonstration purposes, type *me* in the To box.

3. Click an insertion point in the message area, type *Another reminder*, press Enter, and click the Send button on the toolbar.

4. If necessary, click the Send And Receive button so that you can see how a forwarded message looks.

Deleting Messages

In the early days of e-mail, people would often hang onto old e-mail messages so that they had a record of their senders' addresses. Because it is so easy to add e-mail addresses to the Address Book, that particular reason for keeping old messages no longer exists. After you have finished reading many of your messages, you will probably want to delete them. To demonstrate how to delete messages, we'll clean up the Sent Items folder, but bear in mind that the procedure is the same for any folder. Follow these steps:

1. Click the Sent Items icon on the Outlook bar to display the headers of all the messages you have sent. (Outlook Express stores copies of your sent messages in this folder because the Save Copy Of Sent Messages option is selected by default on the Send tab of the Options dialog box.)

The Sent Items icon

2. Choose Select All from the Edit menu and click the Delete button on the toolbar. (You can also hold down the Shift key and click to make selections, the same way you can in My Computer.)

3. Click the Deleted Items icon on the Outlook bar and notice that the deleted files have simply been transferred there, giving you an opportunity to change your mind about deleting them.

The Deleted Items icon

4. You really do want to delete these files, so right-click the Deleted Items icon, choose Empty Folder from the shortcut menu, and click Yes to confirm that you want to discard them.

Emptying the Deleted Items folder

Organizing Messages

When you first started Outlook Express, the program provided five folders: Inbox, Outbox, Sent Items, Deleted Items, and Drafts. In addition to these program-generated folders, you can create your own folders to help organize messages in logical ways. (Some people prefer to create folders for all their messages so that the Inbox folder acts as a temporary receptacle for new messages only.) Let's create a folder and move some messages into it now:

1. Choose Layout from the View menu to display the dialog box shown on page 100. Then, in the Basic section, deselect Outlook Bar and Folder Bar, select Folder List, and click OK.

Creating a new folder

2. Right-click Outlook Express in the folder list and choose New Folder from the shortcut menu to display this dialog box:

3. Type *Staff Party* in the Folder Name edit box and click OK.

4. Click Inbox, select the *Confirm rental* message, and drag it to the Staff Party folder.

Here's another way to move messages:

Sorting messages

You can quickly sort messges in your Inbox by priority, attachment, sender, subject, or the date received by clicking the appropriate header column. Clicking the header again will reverse the sort order (ascending vs. descending). You can also determine a sort order by choosing Sort By from the View menu and choosing the desired options.

1. Right-click the *FW: Confirm rental* message header, choose Move To from the shortcut menu, select the Staff Party folder in the Move dialog box, and click OK.

2. Click Staff Party in the left pane to display the message headers in their new location, like this:

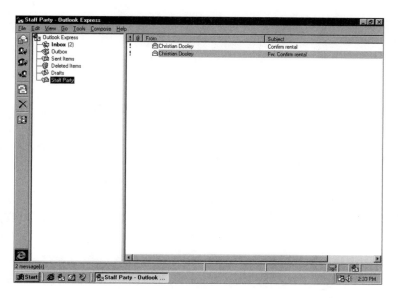

3. Close Outlook Express and if necessary, disconnect from your ISP.

We'll leave you to experiment with folders as you receive mail from your colleagues. That concludes our tour of the Windows 98 e-mail capabilities. You now have plenty of information to conduct your electronic correspondence.

PART TWO

BUILDING PROFICIENCY

In Part Two, we build on the techniques you learned in Part One to round out your Windows 98 skills. After completing these chapters, you will know enough to streamline and personalize Windows 98, as well as troubleshoot common problems. In Chapter 5, you learn several ways to increase your efficiency. In Chapter 6, you learn how to add, remove, and reorganize your Windows setup to suit your own way of working. In Chapter 7, you learn some ways to ward off computer mishaps with basic preventive care.

5
Increasing Your Efficiency

We create shortcut icons for programs and folders on the desktop, and then we add shortcuts to the Start menu, the Programs submenu, and the StartUp submenu. Next, we add toolbars to the taskbar, and finally, we show you some handy techniques for speeding up your everyday tasks.

Create shortcut icons for files, folders, and programs for easy access from the desktop

Create a new, blank document directly on the desktop

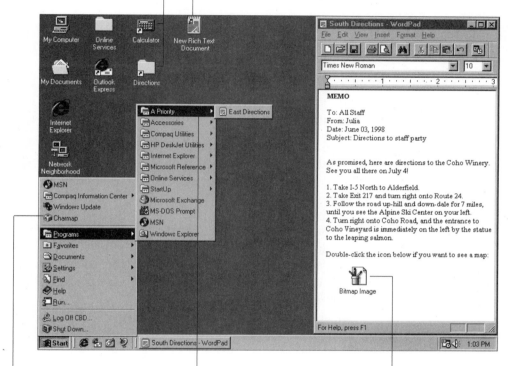

Add shortcuts to the top of the Start menu by dragging icons to the Start button

Create submenus on the Programs menu and then add file, folder, or program shortcuts

Embed one file in another as an icon

Part One showed you how to accomplish basic Windows tasks and gave you enough information to start working in this new environment. By now you've probably experimented a bit, and you're ready to move on to more complex tasks. In this chapter, we focus on how to take advantage of Windows 98 to get your work done efficiently.

Getting Going Quickly

You've learned how to start a program by choosing it from the Programs submenu of the Start menu. You've also learned how to start a program and open a document at the same time using the following methods:

- **The Documents submenu.** Click the Start button, point to Documents, and choose the one you want.

- **The My Computer, Windows Explorer, Network Neighborhood, or Find window.** Locate and double-click the document. (You can also start a program by double-clicking its icon in these windows.)

All of these methods of getting down to work require several steps, but with Windows, you can speed things up by making the programs and documents you use most frequently immediately accessible. In this section, we'll examine a few simple techniques to provide instant access.

Using Shortcut Icons

For ultimate convenience, you can create a shortcut to any program, folder, or document and place an icon representing the shortcut on the desktop. Then double-clicking the icon starts the program, or takes you directly to the folder's window, or opens the document, depending on the nature of the shortcut.

Creating Shortcut Icons

To demonstrate, we'll create a shortcut icon on the desktop for the Calculator program you used in Chapter 2. Follow these steps:

1. Open Windows Explorer, double-click the (C:) icon, and then double-click the Windows icon to display its subfolders and files in the right pane.

Ready-made shortcuts

If you install a new program on your computer, the program's setup utility may create desktop shortcuts and Start menu shortcuts for you. If your desktop and Start menu become cluttered with shortcuts you rarely use, you can discard them without affecting their programs in any way (see pages 121 and 127).

2. If the window is maximized, click the Restore button and then size the window so that you can see the icons on the left side of the desktop.

3. Scroll the right pane until you see the Calc (for *Calculator*) program.

4. Point to the Calc icon, and using the right mouse button, drag a dotted image of the icon onto the desktop, releasing the mouse button when the image is in a blank area.

The Calc icon

5. Choose Create Shortcut(s) Here from the shortcut menu. Windows adds the shortcut icon to the desktop, as shown here:

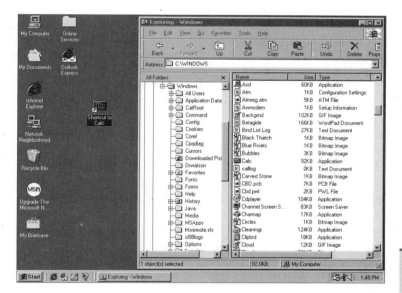

6. The arrow in the bottom left corner of the icon tells you that double-clicking this icon is a shortcut way of starting the program called *Calc*, so you don't need the word *Shortcut* in the name. To change the name, make sure the icon is selected, then click the icon name, type *Calculator*, and press Enter.

Now let's try out the shortcut icon:

1. Double-click the Calculator shortcut icon to display the Calculator window shown earlier on page 43.

The Create Shortcut Wizard

In our example, we select an object and then specify the location for its shortcut icon. But you can also select a location and then specify the object. Simply right-click the desktop or the folder where you want to create the shortcut icon and choose New and then Shortcut from the shortcut menu. Windows starts the Create Shortcut Wizard, and you can then follow the instructions in the wizard's dialog boxes.

2. Click the buttons for 24.95, click *, click 4, and then click =. The display bar shows the cost (without sales tax) of four copies of *Quick Course in Microsoft Office*: 99.8, or $99.80.

3. Close the Calculator by clicking its Close button.

Creating a shortcut icon to a folder or document is just as easy. As an example, let's put the Directions folder and the North Directions document within easy reach:

1. If necessary, scroll the tree diagram in the Exploring window's left pane. Then double-click first the My Documents icon and then the Staff Party icon.

2. Using the right mouse button, drag the Directions folder icon to the desktop, choose Create Shortcut(s) Here from the shortcut menu, and change the name of the shortcut to *Directions*.

3. Double-click the Directions shortcut icon. Windows displays the Directions folder window without you having to go through My Computer and the preceding folder levels.

4. Using the right mouse button, drag the North Directions document icon to the desktop, choose Create Shortcut(s) Here from the shortcut menu, and change the shortcut icon's name to *North Directions*. Here are the results:

Program icons vs. shortcut icons

Shortcut icons are distinguished from program icons by the upward-pointing arrow in the bottom left corner. Whereas program icons visually represent their programs, shortcut icons are instructions to Windows. For example, the program icon for the Calculator is located in the Windows folder on your C drive if that's where the program is stored, and if you move the program to another folder, its icon moves to the new location, too. However, if you create a shortcut icon to the Calculator on the desktop, the icon doesn't indicate that the program itself is stored on the desktop. Instead, the shortcut icon stores the address of the program, and double-clicking the icon tells Windows to go to that address and start the program it finds there. Each program has only one program icon, but you can create many shortcuts to that program and move them wherever you want. And when you no longer need a particular shortcut, you can simply delete it without affecting the program or its other shortcuts in any way.

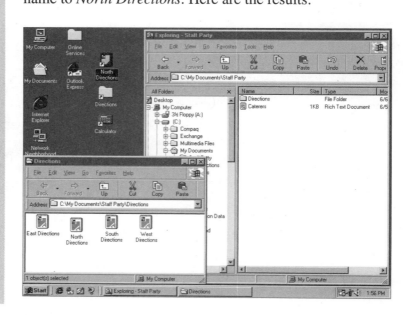

5. Double-click the North Directions shortcut icon. Windows starts your word processor and opens the document. Click the Close button to close the window again.

If you work on a networked computer and often open a file located on another computer, you can create a shortcut icon for it on your desktop by dragging its icon from Network Neighborhood. Then to open the file, you can simply double-click the shortcut icon. If you save changes to the file, Windows knows to save the file on the originating computer.

Shortcuts to network files

You can create shortcut icons within folder windows as well as on the desktop. For example, to create a shortcut icon for the North Directions document in the (C:) window, display both the (C:) and the Directions folder windows, right-drag the North Directions icon from the Directions window into the (C:) window, and then choose Create Shortcut(s) Here from the shortcut menu.

Shortcuts within folders

Deleting Shortcut Icons

When you no longer need immediate access to a program, folder, or document, you can delete its shortcut icon to free up space on the desktop. Here's how:

1. Select the North Directions shortcut icon and press Delete.

2. When Windows asks you to confirm that you want to send the North Directions shortcut icon to the Recycle Bin, click Yes.

3. Close the Directions folder, but leave Explorer open.

Using Start Menu Shortcuts

When you are working in a maximized window, you cannot see the desktop to double-click any shortcut icons you might have placed there. You can either click the Show Desktop button on the Quick Launch toolbar to display the desktop, or you can use the Start menu to access a program or document.

The Show Desktop button

The Start menu is actually a group of shortcuts arranged in a series of submenus. You can add shortcuts to the Start menu itself or to its Programs submenu, as you'll see if you follow the steps on the next page.

1. Double-click the Windows folder icon and scroll the right pane to find the Charmap (for *Character Map*) program.

Adding programs to the top of the Start menu

2. Point to the Charmap icon, and using the left mouse button, drag the dotted image of the icon down onto the Start button in the bottom left corner of the screen. When the Start menu pops up, release the mouse button to add Charmap to the menu, like this:

3. Click the Close button of the Exploring window to both close the Start menu and close the window.

Adding Shortcuts to the Programs Submenu

Suppose you want to create a submenu from which you can easily access all the important documents you are currently working on, including the Directions documents. Here's how you can include this submenu in the Start menu's Programs list and how to add a shortcut for the East Directions document to the new submenu:

Adding submenus to the Start menu

1. Right-click a blank area of the taskbar, choose Properties from the shortcut menu, and click the Start Menu Programs

tab in the Taskbar Properties dialog box to display the options shown here:

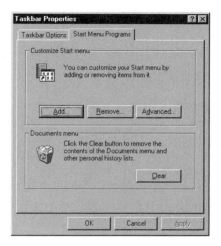

2. Click the Add button. Windows starts the Create Shortcut Wizard, which displays this dialog box:

The Create Shortcut Wizard

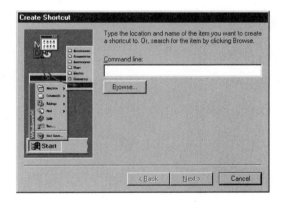

3. If you are an experienced DOS user, you can probably figure out that you need to type *C:\My Documents\Staff Party\Directions\East Directions.rtf* in the Command Line edit box. However, you must enclose the path of the document in quotation marks because the folder and file names include spaces, and you must include its extension. (See the tips on pages 36 and 136 for information about paths and extensions.) For this example, click the Browse button to display the dialog box shown on the next page so that you can look for the document.

Using the Browse dialog box

4. With (C:) displayed in the Look In box, double-click the My Documents icon, then the Staff Party icon, and then the Directions icon.

5. Change the setting in the Files Of Type drop-down list to All Files to display the Directions folder's contents.

6. Finally, double-click the East Directions document to close the Browse dialog box and enter the path of the selected document in the Command Line edit box.

7. Click Next to display this wizard dialog box:

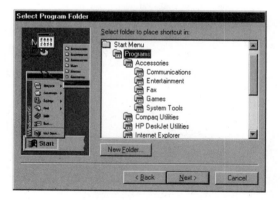

This dialog box displays all the possible locations you can select as a home for a shortcut to the specified document. Notice that Programs is the only first-level submenu of the Start menu to which you can add shortcuts.

8. With Programs selected, click the New Folder button to create a submenu for your documents. The wizard adds a new

subfolder called *Program Group (1)* within the Programs folder and places it in alphabetical order in the subfolder diagram.

9. Type *A Priority* as the new folder's name and then click Next to display the wizard's last dialog box:

Putting the submenu at the
top of the list

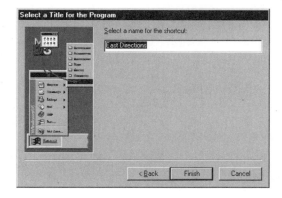

10. Click Finish to accept the suggested shortcut name, and then click OK to close the Taskbar Properties dialog box.

Now for the acid test:

1. Click the Start button to display the Start menu, point to Programs, and then point to A Priority. Here's the shortcut to the document, just waiting to be clicked:

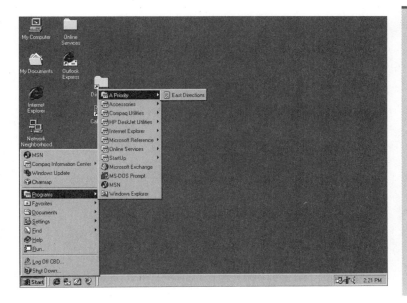

Manually rearranging the Programs submenu

In our example, we named the new folder *A Priority* so that Windows would place the folder at the top of the Programs submenu. However, you can manually rearrange shortcuts on the Programs submenu by selecting a shortcut and dragging it to its new location. As you drag, Windows displays a thick, black line showing where the shortcut will move when you release the mouse button. You can also drag a shortcut from the Programs submenu to the top of the Start menu.

Adding Shortcuts to the StartUp Submenu

When exploring the Start menu, you may have noticed the StartUp submenu and wondered about its purpose. If you use a particular program in almost every computing session, you can have Windows automatically start that program whenever you turn on your computer. All you have to do is put a shortcut to the program in your StartUp folder. Then when you turn on your machine, Windows checks the StartUp folder and starts any programs it contains without you lifting a finger.

To demonstrate, let's put a shortcut to the Calculator program in your StartUp folder. Follow these steps:

Adding programs to the StartUp submenu

1. Click the Start button, point to Settings, choose Taskbar & Start Menu to display the Taskbar Properties dialog box shown earlier on page 123, and click the Start Menu Programs tab.

2. Click Add to start the Create Shortcut Wizard and in the first dialog box, type *C:\Windows\Calc.exe* in the Command Line edit box and click Next. (You don't need to enclose the path in quotation marks because the folder and file names have no spaces.)

3. In the second dialog box, click the StartUp folder at the bottom of the list box and click Next.

4. In the last dialog box, type *Calculator* as the shortcut name and click Finish.

5. Finally, click OK to close the Taskbar Properties dialog box.

To test this StartUp shortcut, you need to restart your computer. Follow these steps:

Restarting your computer

1. Click the Start button and choose Shut Down to display the Shut Down Windows dialog box.

2. Click the Restart option and then click OK. Windows shuts itself down, and then when it finishes restarting, you see the Calculator open on the desktop.

Removing Start Menu Shortcuts

You now have instant access to the Calculator through two shortcuts: the desktop icon and the shortcut on the StartUp submenu. Let's eliminate the redundancy by removing the shortcut from the StartUp submenu (you can also use this technique to remove any shortcut that has been added to the Start menu):

1. Right-click a blank area of the taskbar, choose Properties, and click the Start Menu Programs tab.

2. Click the Remove button to display this dialog box:

3. Double-click the StartUp icon.

4. Select Calculator and click the Remove button.

5. Click Close to close the Remove Shortcuts/Folders dialog box, and click OK to close the Taskbar Properties dialog box. Notice that removing the shortcut from the StartUp menu has not closed the Calculator window, nor has it in any way affected the Calc program stored on your hard drive.

6. Close Calculator.

Rearranging Start menu shortcuts

If you add a shortcut to the Start menu and later decide you want to move it, right-click a blank area of the taskbar and choose Properties from the shortcut menu to open the Taskbar Properties dialog box. Click the Start Menu Programs tab and then click the Advanced button. Windows Explorer starts and configures the Exploring window to display the contents of the Start Menu folder, which is buried deep inside the Windows folder. You can then use normal Explorer techniques (see page 63) to show the contents of subfolders and move, copy, rename, and delete shortcuts.

Using Favorites

If you want to be able to quickly access the documents in a folder but you don't want to clutter up the Start menu with shortcuts, you can add the folder to your list of favorite places. Follow these steps to see how favorites work:

1. Double-click the Directions shortcut on the desktop to display its folder window.

2. Choose Add To Favorites from the Favorites menu to display this dialog box:

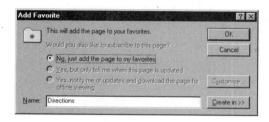

3. Click OK to add the Directions folder to your favorites list.

4. Click the Up button to open the Staff Party folder window, choose Add To Favorites from that window's Favorites menu, and click OK to make the folder a favorite.

5. Close all open windows.

6. Return quickly to the Directions folder by clicking the Start button and choosing Favorites and then Directions from the Start menu.

7. Next, switch to the Staff Party folder by choosing Staff Party from the bottom of the Favorites menu in the Directions folder window.

Web site favorites

In addition to adding folders to your favorites list, if you have Internet access, you can add Web sites. You can also subscribe to a Web site so that you are alerted whenever the site changes. (See Internet Explorer's Help feature for information about how to add and subscribe to Web sites.) The bottom half of the Favorites menu includes predefined Web favorites. Entries for Channels and Links enable you to reach sites on the Channel bar and the Links toolbar by choosing them from the menu. Also included is a Software Updates link that takes you directly to Web sites where you can find new versions of your programs.

Deleting Favorites

We already have a shortcut to the Directions folder on the desktop, so let's delete its favorite:

1. Choose Organize Favorites from the Favorites menu to display this dialog box:

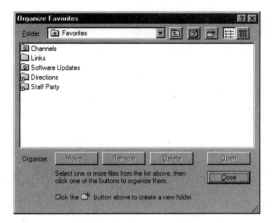

2. Select Directions, press the Delete key or click Delete in the dialog box, confirm the deletion, and then close the dialog box.

The deleted favorite is now in the Recycle Bin. If you decide later that you want it after all, you can open the Recycle Bin and retrieve it. Otherwise, it will be deleted completely when the Recycle Bin is emptied.

Using Taskbar Toolbars

You've seen that the taskbar at the bottom of the screen provides an at-a-glance log of your open tasks, you've used the Start menu as an easy way of opening programs and documents, and you've used a couple of the buttons on the Quick Launch toolbar. In this section, we'll show you how to set up the taskbar so that it provides another way to quickly access the programs or documents you use most often. First, you need to do a little setup work:

1. Double-click the My Documents icon on the desktop to open its window.

2. Right-click a blank area of the window and choose New and then Folder from the shortcut menu. Type *My Programs* as the name of the new folder.

3. Double-click the My Programs icon to open its window.

Customizing taskbar toolbars

If you right-click a taskbar toolbar, Windows 98 opens a shortcut menu giving you several options for changing that toolbar. You can specify whether to show the text of the toolbar buttons, alter the size of the icons, or toggle the toolbar title on and off. Click Open to display a window showing the toolbar's contents, and then you can add and remove programs, shortcuts, and documents as usual. Choose Close from the toolbar shortcut menu to remove the toolbar from the taskbar.

4. Right-click a blank area of the My Programs window and choose New and then Shortcut from the shortcut menu to start the Create Shortcut Wizard. Type *"C:\Program Files\Accessories\Wordpad.exe"* in the Command Line edit box (don't forget the quotation marks), click Next, and then click Finish to store a shortcut to WordPad in the folder.

5. Repeat step 4 to store a shortcut to Paint in the folder, typing *"C:\Program Files\Accessories\Mspaint.exe"* in the Command Line edit box.

6. Close all the open windows.

Adding Toolbars to the Taskbar

Having set up the My Programs folder, you can make its contents available on the taskbar by telling Windows to treat the folder as a toolbar. Follow these steps:

1. Right-click a blank area of the taskbar and choose Toolbars and then New Toolbar from the shortcut menu to display the dialog box shown here:

The Address, Links, and Desktop toolbars

You can display the Address, Links, and Desktop toolbars on the taskbar using the method we describe in the adjacent section. The Address and Links toolbars are visible in many Windows programs, such as My Computer and the Recycle Bin. With the Address toolbar, you can navigate to a folder or file as well as type a Web address to open a Web site without opening a Web browser first. The Links toolbar offers several links to important Web sites. The Desktop toolbar contains all the shortcuts on your desktop, giving you yet another way to access them.

2. Click the plus sign to the left of My Documents, select My Programs to enter its name in the edit box, and click OK.

3. For good measure, repeat steps 1 and 2, this time locating and selecting the Directions folder (which is stored in the Staff Party folder) in the New Toolbar dialog box. Your taskbar now looks like the one shown at the top of the facing page.

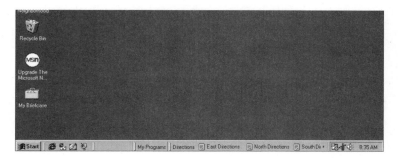

4. As a demonstration, click the East Directions button on the Directions toolbar to start your word processor and open that document. Then close the word processor's window.

Manipulating Taskbar Toolbars

As you can see, the taskbar is now pretty crowded. To the right of the Start button is the familiar Quick Launch toolbar and to the right of that is a blank space reserved for task buttons. Next come truncated My Programs and Directions toolbars. Here are a couple of ways to set up the toolbars for maximum efficiency:

1. To see the entire My Programs toolbar, point to the bar to the left of the word *Directions* and drag to the right. The My Programs toolbar expands and the Directions toolbar contracts, so that they now look like this:

Expanding and contracting toolbars

2. Click the arrow at the right end of the Directions toolbar to scroll the buttons for the documents stored in the Directions folder into view.

3. If you are willing to dedicate more of your screen to the taskbar, you can make it taller. Point to the taskbar's top border

Moving buttons on a toolbar

If you find yourself frequently scrolling to the last button on a toolbar, you can rearrange the buttons for easier access. Point to the desired button, hold down the left mouse button, and drag to place the black I-beam where you want the button to appear. If you close and reopen the toolbar, its buttons will revert to their original order.

and when the pointer changes to a two-headed arrow, drag upward until the taskbar doubles in height. When you release the mouse button, the toolbars spread themselves out, making them easier to read.

Rearranging toolbars

4. Now rearrange the toolbars (this can be tricky!). First, drag the bar to the left of the blank task button area straight down onto the Directions toolbar, which contracts to make room. Then drag the bar to the left of *Directions* to the right of the Wordpad button on the My Programs toolbar. As you can see, the toolbars are now arranged on the top row of the taskbar, and the task buttons have plenty of room on the bottom row:

Let's return the taskbar to its default state:

Turning off taskbar toolbars

1. Right-click a blank area of the taskbar and choose Toolbars and then Directions from the shortcut menu to turn off the Directions toolbar.

2. Repeat step 1 to turn off the My Programs toolbar, noticing that custom toolbars are removed from the shortcut menu when you turn them off. (The default Address, Links, Desktop, and Quick Launch toolbars remain on the menu, even if you turn them off.)

3. Resize the taskbar to its original one row.

Because the taskbar can easily become overcrowded, you have to plan ahead to ensure that any toolbars you add to it increase your efficiency enough to warrant setting them up. For example, you might create a Projects folder containing shortcuts to the documents you are currently working on, or a Log

Floating toolbars

You can add toolbars to the desktop as well as to the taskbar. First create or open the toolbar as usual (see page 130), and then simply drag the toolbar's title onto the desktop, either in the middle or along an edge of the screen. You can then right-click the toolbar and choose Auto Hide or Always On Top to determine whether it appears when windows are maximized.

folder containing shortcuts to mileage or expense reports that you update several times a day. By analyzing your daily tasks, you'll probably find creative ways to use the taskbar to help streamline your work.

Working Smart

Hungry for more ways of speeding up your daily work? This section looks at several techniques for working with documents that take advantage of some nifty built-in Windows capabilities. We'll use the WordPad and Paint programs for our examples, but you can use the same techniques with many commercial programs designed to work with Windows 98.

Creating Instant Documents

You can start a new, blank document with a couple of clicks of the mouse button, without even opening the document's program. Here's how:

1. Right-click a blank area of the desktop and point to New to display a submenu something like the ones shown here:

Creating a new document on the desktop

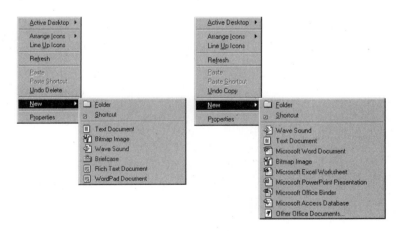

The menu on the left is for a "bare bones" Windows 98 installation, and the one on the right is from a system on which Microsoft Office 97 has been installed. As you can see, the Office programs have been added to the New submenu, so that you can create new Office documents this way.

2. If you have a Rich Text Document item on your submenu, choose it. Otherwise, choose your word processor. Windows displays an icon something like this one on the desktop:

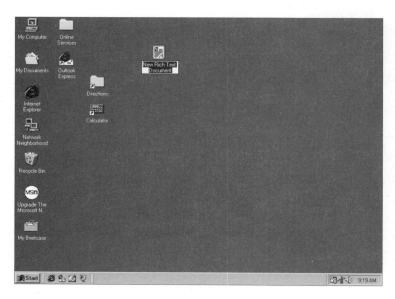

3. Rename the icon as *Map*, retaining the *rtf* extension if it is visible (see page 136 for a discussion of extensions).

4. Double-click the icon. Windows starts your word processor and opens the blank Map document.

5. Type *Here is a map to Adventure Works*.

6. Choose Save As from the File menu, change the Save As Type setting to Rich Text Format if necessary, and click Save. If you are asked whether you want to replace the existing Map document, click Yes.

7. Close your word processor's window.

For good measure, let's create another instant document, this time in a folder:

1. Double-click the Directions shortcut icon on the desktop to display the Directions folder window.

Two documents with the same name?

You may wonder how we can create two files with the exact same name (Map). Actually, the names aren't exactly the same, because the files have different extensions that tell Windows what type of program created the file. For more information about extensions, see the tip on page 136.

2. Right-click a blank area of the folder window and choose New and then Bitmap Image from the shortcut menu. Then rename the icon as *Map*.

3. Double-click the icon to both start your graphics program and open the blank Map graphic document. (If you have no other graphics program, Paint, the program that comes with Windows 98, opens.)

4. If you know how, use the Line, Pencil, and Text tools to create a map something like this one: ◄———

The Line, Pencil, and Text tools

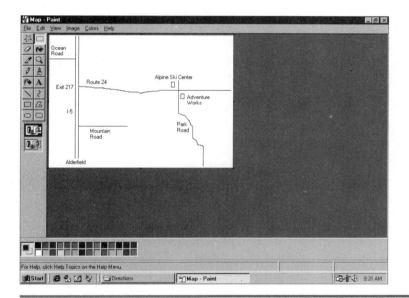

Using Paint's tools

Paint offers lots of tools to help you create your own works of art. Before selecting any tool, first select a color from the color palette at the bottom of the Paint window. Next, click the drawing tool you want in the tool box along the left side of the window. Included are a text tool as well as tools for drawing freehand, straight, and curved lines; painting lines; airbrushing lines; and tools for drawing various geometric shapes. To zoom in for a closer look at a section of your drawing, first click the Magnifier tool and then click the area you want to examine. You can change the zoom percentage by selecting a magnification from the list below the tool box. (This list has different options depending on the tool selected.) To zoom back out, click the Magnifier tool again and then click your drawing. To change an object's color, click the Fill With Color tool, select a color from the color palette, and then click the object. To cut or copy part of a drawing, you can use either the Free-Form Select or Select tools to drag a border around the object, and then choose Cut or Copy from the Edit menu. To erase part of a drawing, use the Eraser tool. If you want to stretch or rotate the drawing, experiment with the commands on the Image menu. If you make a mistake, you can undo the last action by choosing Undo from the Edit menu. To save, open, or print a Paint file, the procedure is the same as in any other Windows program.

You can hold down the Shift key while dragging the Pencil tool to draw straight lines. If you don't know how to work with the Text tool, don't worry about including the street names. The goal here is not to teach you how to use Paint (you can read the tip on the previous page and experiment on your own), but to create a simple graphic for future examples.

5. Save the graphic and close the Paint window.

Next, we'll use the two documents you just created to demonstrate a few other ways to save time by working smarter.

Associating Documents with Programs

The tip way back on page 12 explained that you can often double-click a document's icon to both open the document and start its program because Windows keeps a list of which file types belong to, or are *associated* with, which programs. Sometimes Windows cannot open a document because it has no record of a particular file type. Instead, it displays an Open With dialog box and asks you to select the program you want to use to open the document. And sometimes the list tells Windows to open the document with a different program from the one you want. In either case, you'll need to set the record straight. Follow the steps below to ensure that Rich Text Format documents, which are identified by the *rtf* extension after their file names, are opened with WordPad, and that Bitmap Image documents, which are identified by the *bmp* extension, are opened with Paint. (See the adjacent tip for more information about extensions.)

1. Click the Start button and choose Settings and then Folder Options from the Start menu to display the Folder Options dialog box shown earlier on page 9. (You can also open this dialog box by choosing Folder Options from the View menu of My Computer or Windows Explorer.)

2. Click the File Types tab to display the options shown at the top of the facing page.

Extensions

An extension is a three-character suffix that is added to the end of a file name and separated from the name by a period. Extensions are not case-sensitive; rtf and RTF are the same. Back in the old days when file names were limited to eight characters, extensions were sometimes used to categorize and identify files; for example, *ltr* might be used to identify correspondence. Because you can use long file names in Windows 98, extensions now have a different purpose. Most Windows programs will automatically add a specific extension when you save a file created in that program, and Windows uses this extension to identify which program to open when you double-click the file's icon. (If you manually add a different extension, you will quite often end up with both yours and the program's, separated by periods—and that's not a good idea!) Depending on the settings in the Folder Options dialog box, you may or may not be able to see file extensions. To hide or display extensions, choose Settings and then Folder Options from the Start menu, and then on the View tab, deselect the Hide File Extensions For Known File Types option in the Advanced Settings list.

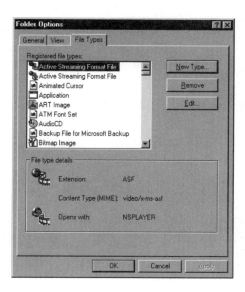

For information about the other options in this dialog box, see the adjacent tip.

3. Scroll the Registered File Types list and select Rich Text Document. The File Type Details section tells you that this file type has an extension of RTF, that its content type is not identified (this information is used by e-mail and Internet programs), and which program will be used to open it.

4. With Rich Text Document selected, click the Edit button to display this dialog box:

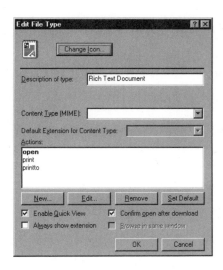

Other File Types options

In addition to editing existing file types by clicking the Edit button, you can also add and remove file types. To add a new file type, click the New Type button. Windows displays the Add New File Type dialog box, where you can enter the specifications of the new file type. To remove a file type from the Registered File Types list, select the type and click the Remove button. Windows then displays a warning asking if you are sure you want to delete the type. If you know you will never need to open files of this type, click Yes.

Selecting an action ──────────▶ 5. Click Open in the Actions list and click Edit again to display yet another dialog box:

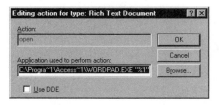

In the Application Used edit box is the path of the program used to open RTF files, followed by "%1". This last part is a programming technique that tells the specified program to open whatever file you double-click. You don't have to worry exactly how this technique works, but you must be sure to include the *"%1"* if you change the entry in this box.

6. Click the Browse button and in the Open With dialog box, double-click Program Files, then Accessories, and then Word-Pad. Back in the Editing Action dialog box, click an insertion point at the right end of the new entry in the Application Used edit box, press the Spacebar, and type *"%1"*.

7. With *"C:\Program Files\Accessories\Wordpad.exe" "%1"* in the Application Used edit box, click OK and then click the Close button.

Other actions

The other actions listed in the Actions list of the Edit File Type dialog box are the default commands that have been defined for the selected file type. Don't mess with these actions unless you're sure you know what you're doing. You can edit an existing command as we explain here, and really techie types can create new commands by clicking the New button. To delete a command, select it in the Actions list and click the Remove button. To reset the list to the default commands, click the Set Default button.

8. If necessary, repeat steps 3 through 7 to associate the Bitmap Image file type's Open action with Microsoft's Paint program. The path in the Application Used edit box should be as follows:

   "C:\Program Files\Accessories\Mspaint.exe" "%1"

9. Click Close to close the Folder Options dialog box.

10. Test your associations by opening and closing the Map.rtf document and the Map.bmp graphic. Then close the Directions folder window.

If necessary, return these associations to their former programs when you have worked your way through the book.

Sending Documents Places

Suppose you want to move the Map document whose icon is now on your desktop to the Directions folder. Because you created a shortcut to the Directions folder window, you can simply drag the Map document icon from the desktop on top of the Directions folder window icon. But for demonstration purposes, we'll show you another way to accomplish the same task, by using the Send To command. (We used this command in Chapter 3 to copy files to a floppy disk; see page 81.) Follow these steps:

1. Open My Computer, click the Address bar, type *C:\Windows\Send To*, and press Enter to display the contents of the SendTo folder window.

← Opening the SendTo folder

2. If necessary, click the window's Restore button and size the window so that you can see all its contents and the Directions shortcut, like this:

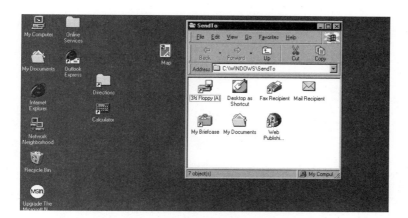

Unassociated files

If you try to open a file that is not associated with a particular program, Windows displays the Open With dialog box. Here, you can select a program from the list, or you can click the Other button and navigate to the desired program. After choosing the program you want to use to open files of that type, click OK to open the file. To make sure that Windows always opens that particular file type with the program you designated, click the Always Use check box before clicking OK. If you are making a permanent association, you will need to fill out the Description edit box with a description of the file type. (You can use whatever wording you like.)

Adding a shortcut to the
SendTo folder

3. Point to the Directions shortcut icon on the desktop, hold down Ctrl, and drag a copy of the icon into the SendTo folder window, releasing first the mouse button and then Ctrl.

4. Close the SendTo window.

5. Now right-click the Map document icon and choose Send To and then Directions from the shortcut menu. The Map icon disappears from the desktop.

6. Double-click the Directions shortcut icon to open its folder window, and verify that the Map document is now stored in this folder.

Reusing Information

If you followed along with the examples in Chapter 2, you know that reusing the same information in different documents is easy. Just select the information in the desired source document, choose Copy from the Edit menu, open the document in which you want to paste the information, click an insertion point, and choose Paste from the Edit menu.

However, the power of Windows 98 far exceeds this simple kind of copying and pasting. With Windows, you can build documents that are patchworks of pieces created in different programs, while maintaining the association of the pieces with the programs that created them. These "patchwork" documents are made possible by a feature called *OLE* (pronounced *olay*). The technology behind OLE is pretty com-

OLE

More about the Send To command

You can use the Send To command as an alternative to associating file types. For example, if you usually want RTF documents to be opened in your word processor but you want to open a particular RTF document in Word-Pad, you can add a WordPad shortcut to your SendTo folder and then use the Send To/WordPad command to open the document instead of double-clicking it. If your SendTo folder contains a shortcut to your printer, you can use the Send To command to send files to the printer without opening them. To set up a printer shortcut, you need to first open the SendTo folder window in My Computer or Windows Explorer. Then click the Start button and choose Settings and then Printers from the Start menu to open the Printers folder window. Arrange the Printers window so that it doesn't obscure the SendTo window, drag the icon for the default printer into the SendTo window, and click Yes when Windows asks if you want to create a shortcut. To print a document using the Send To command, right-click the document you want to print and choose Send To and then your printer from the shortcut menu. Windows then opens the document in its source program, prints the document (you may have to click OK in a dialog box), and closes both the document and the program.

plicated, but you don't have to be an OLE expert to take advantage of it. Here is a quick overview of the concept so that you can decide when and how to use it.

The *O* in OLE stands for *object*. As you know, an object is an item or an element of a document. It can be a block of text, a graphic, a table, a chart, and so on. The program that creates the object is called the *server*, and the original document is called the *source document*. The object can be used by another program called the *client*, and the document in which the object is used is called the *client document* or the *container document*.

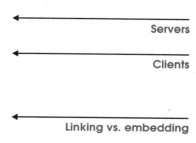

Servers

Clients

Linking vs. embedding

To create a patchwork document, you can *link* an object to the document (the *L* in OLE) or you can *embed* the object (the *E*). When you link an object, you need both the source document and the container document to be able to display the object. When you embed an object, it becomes part of the container document and you no longer need the source document.

So how does all this influence how you go about creating patchwork documents? If the object is used in more than one document and is likely to change, it is best to create the object in its own source document and then link the object where it's needed. If the object is used in only one document or is not going to change, embedding might be the best way to go because embedded information can be edited in the container document without the source document having to be present. Bear in mind, however, that documents that contain embedded objects can get very large.

So that's the scoop on OLE. Now let's see how you might go about using it. First, we'll embed the graphic you created in Paint in a Directions document:

1. In the Directions folder window, double-click the North Directions document to open it in WordPad.

2. Maximize the WordPad window if necessary, press Ctrl+End to move to the end of the document, press Enter, type *Here is a map:*, and press Enter twice.

OLE-supporting programs

Most recent versions of commercial Windows application programs support OLE in some fashion, but not all are capable of acting both as an OLE server and an OLE client, and not all support the most recent incarnation of the OLE technology. If you are working with an older version of a favorite program, you will need to experiment to find out what its capabilities are.

Embedding objects ⟶

3. Choose Object from the Insert menu to display this dialog box:

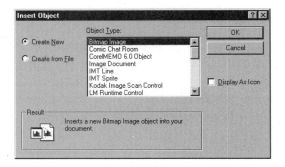

4. With Bitmap Image selected in the Object Type list, select the Create From File option, and when the dialog box changes to let you enter the name of the document, click the Browse button to display the Browse dialog box.

5. Navigate to the Directions folder and then double-click the Map graphic to return to the Insert Object dialog box with the document's path in the File edit box. (If you have trouble with this step, then enter *C:\My Documents\Staff Party\Directions\Map.bmp* in the File edit box.)

6. Click OK. The dialog box closes, and you return to the North Directions document, where the map has been embedded in a large frame, as shown here:

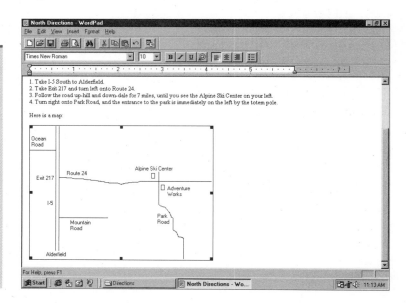

Other programs

Although the instructions given here are specific to WordPad, the procedure is very similar for other Windows application programs that support OLE. To link or embed an object in another program, look for an Object or Insert Object command and follow the directions given in the dialog box, using Help if necessary. (Some programs also forge links by means of a Paste Special command on the Edit menu.)

7. Save the document.

Now suppose you need to change Ocean Road in the map to Ocean Avenue. Instead of making the change in Paint and re-embedding the object in North Directions, you can change it using Paint's tools without leaving WordPad, like this:

1. Double-click the map object. The screen looks like this:

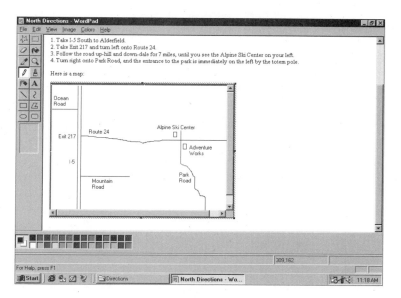

Editing embedded objects

As you can see, the menu bar has changed, and the window has many of the characteristics of a Paint window, even though the title bar shows that you are still in WordPad.

2. If you know how to use the Eraser and Text tools, change Ocean Road to Ocean Avenue. (If you don't, use the Pencil

Creating new objects

When you choose Object from the Insert menu, you have the option of creating a new object of the specified type. For example, clicking OK in the Insert Object dialog box with the Create New option and Bitmap Image selected displays an empty frame in the open North Directions document, and Paint's menus and tools appear. You can then draw the map object directly in the frame. Clicking outside the frame removes Paint's menus and tools but leaves the map object in place as part of the document. You can edit the map later by simply double-clicking it to redisplay Paint's menus and tools.

tool to make a squiggle. You just need to see that when you embed an object, you can change it using the program that created it, even though the object is now stored in another document.)

3. Click outside the graphic's frame, save the document, and then close WordPad.

Instead of embedding the map as a graphic object, you can embed it as an icon. Follow these steps to see the difference:

Embedding an object as an icon

1. Open the South Directions document, press Ctrl+End to move to the end of the document, press Enter, type *Double-click the icon below if you want to see a map:*, and press Enter twice.

2. Choose Object from the Insert menu and with Bitmap Image selected as the object type, select the Create From File option, and type *C:\My Documents\Staff Party\Directions\Map.bmp* in the File edit box.

3. Click the Display As Icon check box, and click OK. Here's the result:

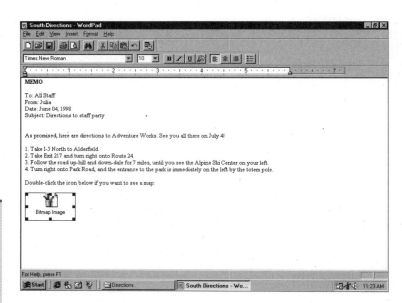

What exactly are you editing?

When you make changes to an embedded object (one that is not linked to its source document), you are changing the version of the object that is stored in the open container document. Your changes do not in any way affect the original source document.

4. Save the document and then double-click the icon. A Paint window opens displaying nothing but the map. Notice that the original Map graphic was not affected by the changes you

made to the map object in the North Directions document. (See the tip on the facing page.)

5. Choose Exit & Return To South Directions from the File menu to return to your document.

6. Close the WordPad window.

Now let's link the map to two different documents, first as a graphic object and then as an icon:

1. Open the East Directions document, press Ctrl+End, press Enter, type *Here is a map:*, and press Enter twice.

Linking an object

2. Choose Object from the Insert menu, and with Bitmap Image selected in the Object Type list, select the Create From File option, and then type *C:\My Documents\Staff Party\Directions\Map.bmp* in the File edit box.

3. Click the Link check box and click OK.

4. Save the document.

5. Click the Open button on the toolbar and in the Open dialog box, navigate to the Directions folder. Select Rich Text Format from the Files Of Type drop-down list, and then double-click West Directions to open that document.

The Open button

6. Press Ctrl+End, press Enter, type *Double-click the icon below if you want to see a map:*, and press Enter twice.

7. Choose Object from the Insert menu and with Bitmap Image selected as the Object Type, select Create From File and type *C:\My Documents\Staff Party\Directions\Map.bmp* in the File edit box.

Linking an object as an icon

8. Click both the Link and Display As Icon check boxes, and then click OK. A shortcut icon to the Map graphic now appears at the bottom of the document.

9. Save the document and close the WordPad window.

Now suppose that Exit 217 on the map should be Exit 216. Because the map in the East Directions and West Directions documents is linked to the source Paint document, you can edit the Map graphic in Paint and the change will be reflected in the two linked documents. Follow these steps:

Editing the source document

1. Double-click the Map graphic icon in the Directions folder to open the map in Paint. Use the Eraser and Text tools to make the necessary changes (or make a squiggle or two with the Pencil tool), save the map, and close Paint.

2. Open the East Directions document. Windows displays a message box stating that it is updating ActiveX objects. When the message box disappears, scroll the window.

3. If the linked object doesn't reflect the changes you made to the Paint document, choose Links from the Edit menu to display this dialog box:

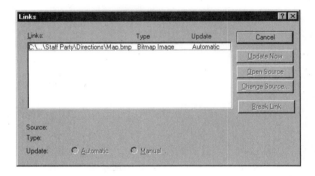

4. Select the link to the Map graphic, click Update Now, click Close, and then save the document.

5. Now open the West Directions document by choosing it from the File menu. (Most Windows programs store the names of the documents you worked with most recently at the bottom of the File menu so that you can quickly access them again.)

6. Double-click the Map icon. You move to a Paint window with the new version of the map displayed.

7. Tidy up the desktop by closing all open windows, saving any changes if prompted.

What are ActiveX objects?

ActiveX objects are used primarily by Internet Explorer but also by Windows 98 to add dynamic, interactive elements to documents. You can think of ActiveX objects as mini-programs, or *applets*, that perform discreet functions. In this case, the object's function is related to the updating of the linked graphic.

Depending on the programs you are using, you may find that OLE sometimes doesn't work quite as well as you would like. Or you may find that it works well under certain circumstances, such as when the source document is open, and not so well under others, such as when the source document is closed. However, if you need to create dynamic documents that contain objects from different programs, it is worth taking the time to experiment with OLE so that you understand how it works in the particular programs you use.

That's it for this chapter on efficiency. Hopefully, being aware of some of the possibilities will help you make your time at the computer more productive.

6 Customizing the Way You Work

We discuss how to add hardware and install programs, how to set up the screen the way you want it, and how to customize the taskbar. Then we cover other common adjustments that you can use to tailor your computer to your own way of working.

*Customize the taskbar
in a variety of ways*

*Use Control Panel icons to
tailor your computer setup
to the way you work*

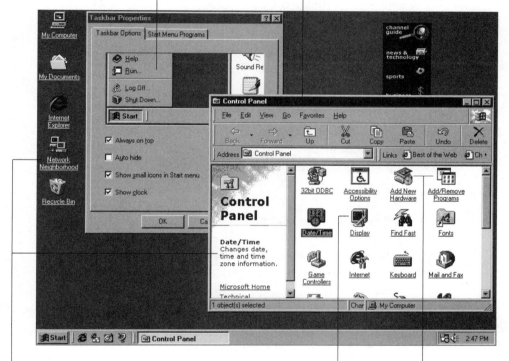

*Make the desktop and
My Computer work like a
Web page by switching
to Web style*

*Change screen colors, run
a screen saver, and make
other display adjustments*

*Add hardware and
install new programs
with the help of wizards*

In this chapter, we give you a brief overview of the Windows 98 tools you can use to change your computer's setup in a variety of ways. We've left this discussion until Chapter 6 because we feel you are unlikely to need these tools when you first start using Windows. Moreover, if you are working on a network, your network administrator may not allow you to make some changes. No matter what your particular situation, you can look through this chapter to learn about the available options. Then if you're allowed to experiment, you'll know where to start.

First, we'll briefly discuss how to add or remove hardware and programs.

Adding or Removing Hardware

If you add new hardware to your computer, such as a sound card, modem, or CD-ROM drive, you will want Windows to recognize this new device. Windows 98 features *Plug and Play* technology, which makes adding new hardware easier. With Plug and Play, you still have to physically attach new hardware to your computer, but you no longer have to fuss around with drivers and setup programs. When you turn on your computer, Windows 98 recognizes the new device, takes care of setting it up, and installs any programs necessary to make the new hardware work, prompting you for files if necessary.

Plug and Play

Sounds great, right? Unfortunately, there's a snag. To take full advantage of this technology, you must have Plug and Play support in these areas:

Plug and Play requirements

• **Your computer's BIOS.** The BIOS (basic input-output system) is a program built into your computer that you usually don't have to worry about. However, if you upgrade an older computer to Windows 98, the BIOS may not support Plug and Play. If you purchase a computer with Windows 98 already installed or you upgrade a relatively new computer from Windows 95, then the BIOS should have Plug and Play support (check your computer's documentation).

- **The hardware device.** Any new hardware device you buy supports Plug and Play if it has the Windows 95 or Windows 98 logo on the box. Microsoft allows hardware manufacturers to display this logo only if the hardware has Plug and Play capability.

For those of you with older computers, all is not lost. Windows 98 includes an Add New Hardware Wizard that makes adding a new device easier than it was with previous versions of Windows. To use this wizard, you choose Settings and then Control Panel from the Start menu, and double-click the Add New Hardware icon in the Control Panel window. The wizard displays a series of dialog boxes asking you questions about the new device. Armed with this information, Windows can search for any Plug and Play devices and display a list of any it finds. To have Windows try to determine the correct settings and install the correct driver, select the device you want to add and click Next. Then follow the wizard's instructions to complete the process.

The Add New Hardware icon

If Windows can't locate the new device, the wizard displays a dialog box in which you can select the hardware type, make, and model. Windows can then usually install the new hardware correctly.

If the hardware you are adding is not listed in the wizard's dialog box and a driver did not come with it, contact the device's manufacturer and ask for a Windows 98 driver and the instructions for installing it.

If you upgrade a hardware device or completely remove a device from your computer, here's how to tell Windows that the old device is no longer available:

Removing hardware

1. Open Control Panel, double-click the System icon in the Control Panel window, and then click the Device Manager tab to display the options shown on the following page.

The System icon

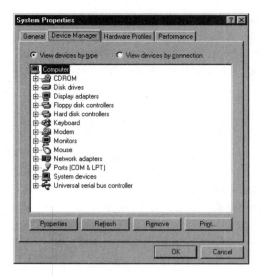

USB and FireWire support

One of the new features of Windows 98 is support for the USB and FireWire technologies. USB stands for *universal serial bus* and defines a type of hardware that makes adding multiple serial devices to your computer much easier. FireWire is a peripheral bus defined by IEEE 1394, and is similar to USB but works at a higher speed. The main advantages of the technologies are that they each use a standard connector type and that you can chain devices together. (USB and FireWire connections cannot be interchanged.) To install a USB or FireWire device, simply plug the cord from the device into a compatible port. (You can attach and detach devices while your computer is running.) Windows will recognize the device and install the appropriate driver for it.

Before we go any further, here's a word of warning: don't play around where Windows and devices are concerned. Using this dialog box to tell Windows that you have removed a hardware device is relatively straightforward, but unless you know what you're doing, don't mess with the settings in this dialog box for any other reason.

2. Check that the View Devices By Type option is selected and then double-click the type of hardware you have removed to display a list of makes and models.

3. Select the make and model of the device, click the Remove button, and then click OK.

Adding or Removing Programs

Gone are the days when adding a program to your computer was a simple matter of copying the program to your hard drive. Nowadays, each application includes a setup or installation program that makes sure all the necessary pieces are copied to the correct locations and alerts Windows to their existence. If you later remove the application, not only must its files be deleted from your hard drive, but ideally Windows should remove all references to the application from its system files. Similarly, if you add or remove any programs that come with Windows 98, Windows needs to be involved so that it can take care of the necessary housekeeping.

Adding or Removing Application Programs

To install a new application program from a floppy disk or CD-ROM, open the Control Panel window and double-click the Add/Remove Programs icon to display this dialog box:

The Add/Remove Programs icon

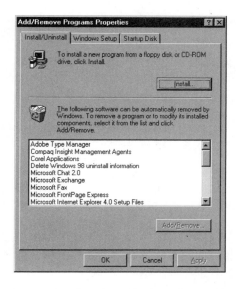

Insert the first installation disk or the CD-ROM and click the Install button to start the Install Wizard. The wizard searches your floppy drive and your CD-ROM drive for a setup program and then prompts you to confirm that it should run the program. When you click Finish, the setup program takes over from the Install Wizard, prompting you for any information it needs.

The Install Wizard

If the application program comes with an uninstall utility, the Install Wizard adds the program to a list of programs that can be removed. If you want to remove the program, you can select it from the list box at the bottom of the Install/Uninstall tab of the Add/Remove Programs Properties dialog box, and then click the Add/Remove button. If the program you want to remove is not listed, look for an uninstall application in the folder where the program is stored. (It will most likely be labeled *Remove* or *Uninstall*.) If you don't find anything there,

Removing programs

check the program's documentation or call technical support for that particular program.

Adding or Removing Windows Components

When Windows 98 was installed on your computer, the person responsible for installing it could pick and choose among various Windows components. As a result, it is unlikely that you have all the programs that come with Windows on your computer. As you work with Windows, you may find you need a program that was not initially installed, or you may find you never use a program that was installed. With Windows, you can add or remove certain components at any time, provided you have permission to change your computer's setup in this way.

Follow these steps to see how to add or remove a component:

1. Double-click the Add/Remove Programs icon in the Control Panel window and then click the Windows Setup tab of the Add/Remove Programs Properties dialog box. After checking your computer for installed components, Windows displays these options:

AutoPlay

When you insert a CD-ROM in your CD-ROM drive, Windows assumes you want to use that CD-ROM immediately. Without you having to do anything, Windows reads the information on the CD-ROM and may display a window with instructions for accessing the CD-ROM's contents. If the window includes a setup program, you can double-click that option to install the program, instead of using the Install Wizard. (Only CD-ROMs that have been produced since the release of Windows 95 in August 1995 can take advantage of the AutoPlay feature.)

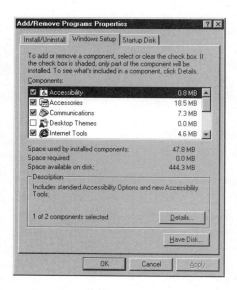

In the Components list, Windows displays its optional components by category. Categories with all components installed display a ✔ in a white check box, while categories with only some components installed display a ✔ in a gray check box. If a category has more than one component, Windows tells you how many components in the selected category are currently installed and how many are available. On the right side of the Components list, Windows displays how much hard disk space the installed components for each category use.

To add or remove an entire category, click the check box to the left of the category's name. (Clicking an empty check box puts a ✔ in the box and adds the category; clicking a check box with a ✔ removes the ✔ and removes the category.)

Adding/removing categories

2. Click the Accessories category name to select that category. (Don't click the check box or you will deselect the entire category.)

3. Click the Details button to display this dialog box:

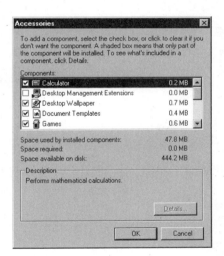

4. If there is no ✔ in the Desktop Wallpaper check box, click the check box to add that component.

Desktop wallpaper

5. Click OK to close the Accessories dialog box, and then click OK once again to close the Add/Remove Programs Properties dialog box.

6. If Windows needs the installation CD-ROM to carry out the command, insert the disk and click OK. Windows copies the necessary files, and desktop wallpaper patterns are now available for you to use (see page 158).

Tailoring the Display

The Display icon

You can tailor the look of your screen by changing its resolution, color scheme, screen saver, and other visual settings. You make these adjustments in the dialog box that appears when you double-click the Display icon in the Control Panel window, but here's a faster way to access this dialog box:

1. Close the Control Panel window, right-click a blank area of the desktop, and choose Properties from the shortcut menu.

2. Click the Settings tab to display these options:

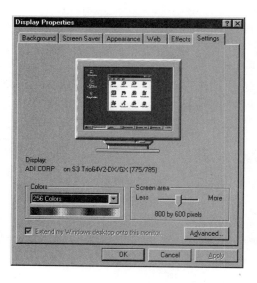

Changing the Number of Colors and the Resolution

The options available on the Settings tab of the Display Properties dialog box reflect the capabilities of your monitor and video card, which are specified below the image of the screen. Here's how to check the possibilities and change the settings if necessary:

1. In the Colors section, click the arrow to the right of the edit box to see the available options, and then click whichever option is already highlighted to retain the existing setting. (You can experiment with different color settings later.)

2. In the Screen Area section, make a note of the current setting. Then drag the slider to the left or right to reduce or increase the screen resolution, and click Apply. You see this dialog box:

3. Click OK, and then click Yes or No when Windows asks if you want to keep the new setting.

Changing the Background

You can easily change the pattern of your desktop or add a picture or an HTML document as background *wallpaper*. (Large, colorful wallpaper files can really eat up memory, so you might want to skip the wallpaper.) First, let's change the pattern of the desktop:

1. Click the Background tab of the Display Properties dialog box to display these options:

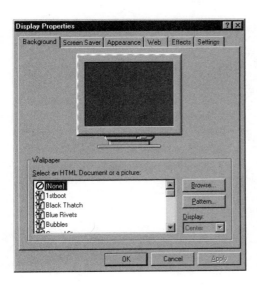

Advanced display settings

On the Settings tab of the Display Properties dialog box, you can click the Advanced button to open a more detailed Properties dialog box. On the General tab, you can alter the appearance of fonts, enable a Display Settings icon on your taskbar, and specify whether to restart the computer after you change settings. On the remaining tabs, you can change your adapter, Plug and Play options, how your graphics hardware components are used, and the default color profile for your monitor.

Adding a pattern **2.** Click the Pattern button to display this dialog box:

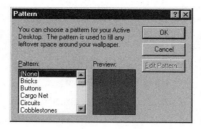

3. Click the various pattern names in the list and notice their effect on the sample screen shown to the right of the list. When you have finished exploring, select Thatches and click OK.

4. Back in the Display Properties dialog box, click Apply to see the effect of the new desktop pattern.

Now let's try wallpapering the background with a graphic:

Adding wallpaper **1.** In the Wallpaper list, click some of the wallpaper names, noticing their effect on the sample screen. Then click Bubbles.

2. Click the arrow to the right of the Display box at the bottom of the dialog box, and select Tile so that the entire desktop will be filled with tiled copies of the wallpaper graphic you have selected. Then click OK. Notice that the wallpaper completely obscures the Thatches pattern you selected earlier.

Power management

To reduce power consumption of your computer, you can choose a *power scheme*, a collection of settings for power usage. Choose Settings and then Control Panel, and then double-click the Power Management icon. Then, on the Power Schemes tab, you can select an existing set of options or you can modify the settings and save a new scheme. On the Advanced tab, you can enable a power meter on the taskbar, or you can request a password-prompt when your computer goes off standby mode.

Desktop themes

By using one of the desktop themes that ship with Windows 98, you can make your desktop, wallpaper, and mouse pointer follow the same theme. Simply double-click the Desktop Themes icon in the Control Panel window and select the one you want to use from the Themes drop-down list. (If the Control Panel window does not contain a Desktop Themes icon, you need to install the themes before you can use them. Follow the instructions on page 154 for installing Windows components.) You can preview the screen saver, pointers, and sounds associated with a theme by clicking the buttons in the Previews section; and you can turn particular components of the theme on or off by clicking the check boxes in the Settings section. Click OK when you are satisfied with your choices. Bear in mind that desktop themes are memory hogs; you may not want to use them if you are low on memory.

3. If you don't like your screen's new look, redisplay the Display Properties dialog box and try a different background, or return the Pattern and Wallpaper settings to (None) as we did.

Displaying a Screen Saver

Using the Display Properties dialog box, you can specify whether Windows should display a moving picture or pattern during periods of screen inactivity. A moving display helps prevent static screen objects, such as window title bars and menu bars, from "burning into" the monitor, saves power during periods of inactivity, and hides your work-in-progress from passersby. Here's how to activate a screen saver:

1. Open the Display Properties dialog box and click the Screen Saver tab to display these options:

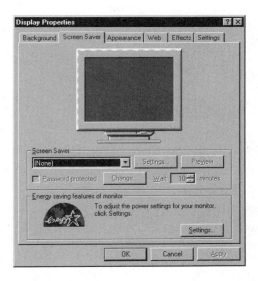

2. Click the arrow at the right end of the Screen Saver box and select 3D Flower Box from the list of options. The sample screen shows what the screen saver looks like, but you can also click the Preview button to see its effect full-screen. (After you click the Preview button, moving the mouse returns you to the Display Properties dialog box.)

3. Watching a flying object might give you motion sickness, so click the Settings button to display the dialog box shown on the following page.

Using other screen savers

You can display a screen saver program that you've purchased or downloaded, by using the Add/Remove Programs icon (see page 153) in the usual way. Then you activate the screen saver by double-clicking the Display icon in Control Panel and selecting the new saver from the drop-down list on the Screen Saver tab.

4. Experiment with the options in this dialog box, clicking OK to view their effects in the Display Properties sample screen. When the screen saver is the way you want it, use the spinner in the Wait edit box to specify 5 minutes as the period of inactivity after which Windows should turn on the screen saver. (Click the up arrow to increment the counter and the down arrow to decrement it.) Then click OK to apply your changes and close the dialog box.

Changing the Color Scheme

To make the screen easy on your eyes, you can change the colors of standard Windows elements, such as the desktop and the active title bar. Follow these steps:

Setting up user profiles

If more than one person uses your computer, you can set up different user profiles so that the settings displayed depend upon the password used when someone logs on to your computer. First, double-click the Passwords icon in Control Panel. Click the User Profiles tab, check that the Users Can Customize Their Preferences setting is selected, and click OK. Then double-click the Users icon in Control Panel and follow the wizard's instructions to create a user profile.

Scrolling text screen saver

Windows provides a screen saver called 3D Text that displays words on your screen when the screen saver is activated. You can use this feature to remind yourself of an important event or a task that needs to be completed during the day. (Obviously, the computer must be turned on and idle for the screen saver to be activated.) To create a text screen saver, select 3D Text from the Screen Saver drop-down list on the Screen Saver tab of the Display Properties dialog box, and then click the Settings button. Type up to 16 characters in the Text edit box (for example, *Joyce's birthday*) and then adjust the size, speed, resolution, and spin style of the text. You can click the Choose Font button to change the font and style of the text. Click OK to return to the Display Properties dialog box, where you can preview the text screen saver before putting it into effect.

1. Open the Display Properties dialog box and click the Appearance tab to display these options:

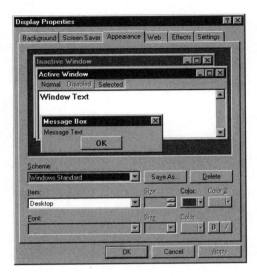

2. Click the arrow to the right of the Scheme box and select Desert from the list of preset color schemes. In the window above the list, Windows shows how the screen will look with that color scheme.

3. Click the arrow to the right of the Item box and select Menu from the list. Then click the arrow to the right of the Color box and select pale gray in the top row of the palette.

4. Next, click the Active Window title bar in the preview window. The setting in the Item box changes to Active Title Bar. Change the color to purple (the last option in the fourth row of the color palette). Then change the font of the active title bar by selecting Times New Roman from the Font drop-down list. Then change the size to 11 and the color to yellow.

5. To save your custom color scheme, click the Save As button, type *!Mine*, and click OK. (Preceding the name with an exclamation mark ensures that the new scheme will appear before Brick at the top of the Scheme drop-down list.)

6. Click OK to implement the new color scheme, or click Cancel to ignore it and leave the current scheme in place.

Using multiple monitors

Windows 98 supports the use of more than one monitor at a time on your computer. For example, you might want to use multiple monitors if you receive e-mail constantly throughout the day and don't want to interrupt the work you are doing to read it. Multiple monitors are also useful for desktop publishing and presentation graphics. Multiple monitors can be used only if all display adapters are PCI or AGP devices. For specific instructions on setting up multiple monitors, see Windows 98 Help. Once you have set up multiple monitors, you can customize the display by opening the Display Properties dialog box and making adjustments on the Settings tab.

Reverting to the default
color scheme

Playing with colors can be fun, and we encourage you to experiment with this feature. To return to the default color scheme,
select Windows Standard from the Scheme drop-down list.

We recommend that you choose colors that are easy on the
eyes, especially if you use Windows a lot. If you have a visual
impairment, you can easily create a high-contrast screen by
using the Accessibility Properties dialog box (see page 176).

Switching to Web Style

Way back in Chapter 1, we had you set your screen to Classic
style to ensure that our instructions would work predictably
for everyone. By doing this, we ignored one of the features of
Windows 98 that sets it apart from previous versions of the
operating system: its tight integration with the Internet. A discussion of the Internet and of the Windows 98 Internet capabilities is beyond the scope of this book, but we do want to
show you how to customize your screen to take advantage of
Internet integration. Then if you have Internet access, you can
experiment on your own.

The Windows 98 Internet capabilities are built around the fact
that you can treat items on your desktop the way you treat them
on a Web page (*Web style*), as well as treating them the way
you always have (*Classic style*). Let's switch to Web style now:

1. Choose Settings and then Folder Options from the Start menu
   to display the dialog box shown earlier on page 9.

2. Click the Web Style option and then click OK.

3. If you see this dialog box:

click OK. Your desktop changes to look like this:

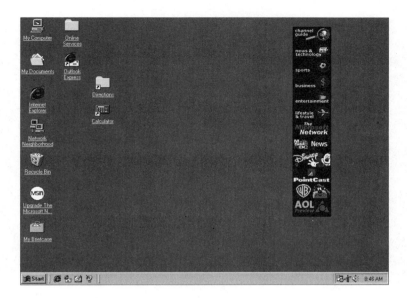

As you can see, all the icon names are now underlined to identify them as *hot links* to programs or folders stored on your computer (or your network). Windows also displays the Channel bar to provide easy access to Web sites you might want to check regularly. (See the adjacent tip for more information about channels.

Now let's see how Web style differs from Classic style. To keep our commentary to a minimum, we'll avoid pointing out the obvious, but notice the subtle and not-so-subtle differences as you follow along with these steps:

1. Point to the My Computer icon, noticing that the pointer changes to a hand and the icon's name changes its color to indicate that it is selected. (With Web style, simply pointing to something selects it; you don't have to click.)

2. Click the icon to open the My Computer window and if necessary maximize the window.

3. Point to the (C:) icon in the My Computer window to select the drive. The window changes to look like the one shown on the following page.

Channels

When Web style is turned on, you can display the Channel bar on your desktop. The Channel bar provides buttons for categories of Web sites, or channels, that offer a wide variety of information. Clicking a button displays icons for the channels in that category. Clicking an icon displays a preview page, giving you a better idea of that channel's content. You can subscribe to any channel, and its content will be downloaded regularly to your computer, giving you up-to-date content directly on your desktop. To learn more about subscribing to channels, see Windows 98 Help.

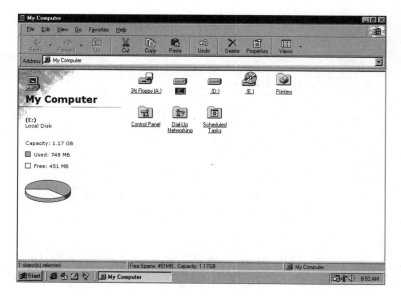

4. Without moving the mouse, click the (C:) icon to display its contents in the same window. Notice that the icon in the same position as the (C:) icon is now selected in the new folder window because you haven't moved the mouse.

5. Point to Windows to transfer the selection to that folder, and then click the Windows icon to open its window, like this:

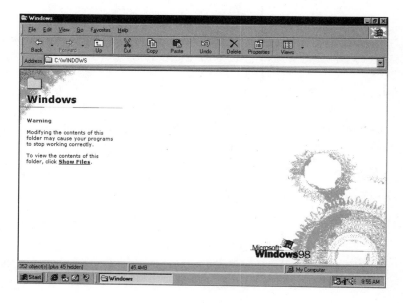

As you can see, with Web style, Windows can provide information to guide you as you use the operating system. The words *Show Files* are underlined and in a different color to indicate that clicking those words will carry out the indicated action.

6. To see the contents of the Windows folder, click Show Files.

7. Scroll all the way to the bottom of the window and select the first file icon in the last full row. Then hold down the Shift key, move the pointer over to the third file icon, release the Shift key, and move the pointer to a blank area of the screen. All three files are now selected.

Selecting multiple files in Web style

8. Now hold down the Ctrl key, point to the second file icon, release the Ctrl key, and move the pointer to a blank area. The results are shown here:

Once you have selected a file or folder, you can move, copy, or delete it in the usual way (but don't try this with the files and folders in the Windows folder or you will almost certainly mess up your system).

CAUTION!

9. Choose My Computer from the Go menu to redisplay the My Computer window.

When Web style is active, point and click actions work the same way in Windows Explorer.

Internet Access Everywhere

My Computer's View, Go, and Favorites menus include commands that are designed to put the resources of the Internet or an organization's intranet at your fingertips. Follow these steps to try some of these commands:

Displaying the Links toolbar →

1. Choose Toolbars and then Links from the View menu. The Links toolbar joins the regular toolbar and the Address bar at the top of the window.

2. Point to the gray bar to the left of the word *Links* and drag to the left until the bars at the top of the window look like this:

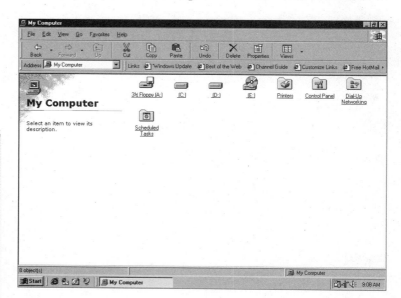

Intranets

Using Internet technology, many companies are setting up Internet servers and creating intranets that are accessible only from the company's computers (no matter where they are physically located). The intranet enables people to easily and cheaply access company information, exchange ideas, and collaborate on projects. A system of security "firewalls" ensures that the intranet information is available only to the people in the company who are authorized to access it, not to general Internet users.

3. Run the pointer slowly over the buttons on the Links toolbar to display description boxes that contain Web addresses known as *URLs* (universal resource locators). Clicking one of these buttons starts Internet Explorer, which jumps to the specified

Web site. (If you click one of these buttons while you're not connected to the Internet, one or more dialog boxes may appear. For now, close the dialog boxes without making any changes, or select the option to stay offline.)

4. Choose Explorer Bar and then Channels from the View menu. (Again, if you see a message box prompting you to connect, continue working offline.) The window splits into two panes with the Explorer bar on the left displaying categories of available channels, as shown here:

Displaying the Explorer bar

We briefly explain channels in the tip on page 163. The idea here is to show you yet another way in which Windows 98 makes a seamless connection between your daily work and the Web.

5. Choose other commands from the Explorer Bar submenu, finishing up with None, which closes the bar.

6. If you are connected to the Internet, take a moment to explore the buttons on the Links toolbar and the commands on the Go and Favorites menus, which also provide one-click access to the Web.

Internet Explorer

Internet Explorer, the Microsoft Web browser, allows you to access information on the World Wide Web. This browser is included with Windows 98 and can be accessed by double-clicking its icon on the desktop. Windows also opens Internet Explorer when you click buttons or Web sites on the Links toolbar in any window, or type a Web address in the Address bar. (See the tip on page 130 for more information about these toolbars.) Obviously, to use Internet Explorer, you need to have an Internet connection set up on your computer. If you want more information on how to use Internet Explorer, you may want to check out *Quick Course in Microsoft Internet Explorer 4*, another book in the Quick Course series.

Reverting to the Traditional Display

Before you continue on with this chapter, switch back to Classic style so that your screens will look the same as ours:

1. Choose Folder Options from the View menu to display the dialog box shown earlier on page 9.

2. Click the Classic Style option and then click OK.

3. Close My Computer.

Customizing the Taskbar

As you have seen while working through the examples in this book, the Start menu and the taskbar are important elements of the Windows 98 interface. Because you use them so frequently, you can customize them for maximum convenience. You learned how to add and remove Start menu items and how to add toolbars to the taskbar in Chapter 5 (see pages 121 and 130). Here, we'll look at ways to manipulate the taskbar itself.

Relocating the Taskbar

Although the taskbar is located at the bottom of your screen by default, it doesn't have to stay there. Try this:

1. Point to a blank area of the taskbar, hold down the left mouse button, and drag to the top of the screen. When you release the mouse button, the taskbar jumps into place, as shown here:

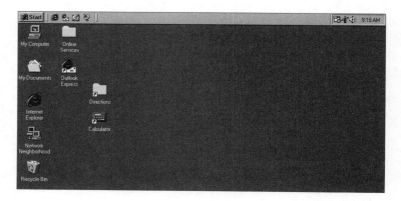

2. Now drag the taskbar to the right side of the screen. Windows adjusts the width of the bar so that you can see the entire Start button.

3. Drag the taskbar back to the bottom of the screen. When you release the mouse button, the taskbar returns to its original size.

Restoring the taskbar

Changing Taskbar Properties

As well as changing the location of the taskbar, you can change its look. Follow these steps:

1. Right-click the taskbar and choose Properties from the shortcut menu to display this dialog box:

2. On the Taskbar Options tab, click the Always On Top check box to deselect it, and notice that the window in the sample screen now overlaps the taskbar.

3. Click the check box again to turn it back on, and notice that the taskbar in the sample screen is now over the window. (You will probably want to leave this option selected so that the taskbar is always at hand.)

4. Click the Auto Hide check box and notice that the taskbar has disappeared from the sample screen. This option is useful when you want to display as much of your document as possible on the screen.

Hiding the taskbar

5. Click OK to close the dialog box.

6. Double-click the My Computer icon and notice that the window fills the entire screen. Point to the bottom edge of the screen, and the taskbar pops up. Move the pointer elsewhere, and the taskbar hides itself.

7. Close My Computer and display the taskbar. Click the Start button, and choose Settings and then Taskbar & Start Menu from the Start menu to redisplay the Taskbar Properties dialog box.

8. Click the Auto Hide check box to turn it off, but leave the dialog box open.

The Taskbar Options tab provides a couple of other ways to tailor the taskbar. Try this:

Changing the Start menu's icons

1. Click the Show Small Icons In Start Menu check box, noticing the effect in the sample screen. Then click the check box again. As you can see, small icons take up less room and large icons are easier to identify. Finish with whichever setting you prefer.

Turning off the clock

2. Toggle the Show Clock check box on and off, noticing the effect in the sample screen. (You might want to turn off the clock if you have many windows open and you want to make room for their buttons on the taskbar.)

3. Check that all the taskbar customization options are as you want them and click OK to close the dialog box.

Other Adjustments

With Windows 98, you rarely need to live with a setting that annoys you or interferes with your work. Do you travel across time zones and need to adjust your computer's clock? Do you want to switch the left and right mouse buttons? Is your keyboard's repeat rate too fast or too slow? Then this section is for you. We'll explore two categories of customization: first, the options you are most likely to want to change and are most likely to be able to experiment with; and second, the options that you are unlikely to want to change and that only experienced users should mess with (provided, of course, that they have the proper permissions).

Many of the adjustments we discuss in the following sections are made using tools available in the Control Panel window. As you'll see, we don't deal with the tools in the order in which they appear in Control Panel, and we don't deal with some of the more techie ones at all. But by the end of this chapter, you'll have a good idea of the range of customization possibilities available to you and of where to look when you want to change something.

Some of the options we cover here are fairly easy to change, and experimenting with them can't harm your system. (As you work through the following examples, bear in mind that you can actually implement a change by clicking OK or pressing Enter in a dialog box, or you can leave the current setting as it is by clicking Cancel or pressing the Esc key.) Other options we discuss here are more obscure, and you might rarely or perhaps never need to change them. If you want, you can just skim through this section, coming back to specific parts if you need to later.

Changing the Date or Time

As you have seen, the time is displayed in the clock at the right end of the taskbar, and the date is displayed in a pop-up box when you point to the time with the mouse. You can use the Date/Time icon in the Control Panel window to set your computer's date and time. Or you can simply right-click the clock at the right end of the taskbar and then choose the Adjust Date/Time command from the shortcut menu. Let's try the second method:

The Date/Time icon

1. Right-click the clock at the right end of the taskbar.

2. Choose Adjust Date/Time from the shortcut menu. Windows displays this dialog box:

3. On the Date & Time tab, click the arrow at the right end of the Month box and select January from the drop-down list.

4. In the Year edit box, click the spinner's up arrow until the year changes to 2000.

5. On the calendar, click Saturday, the 1st.

6. If the time needs adjustment, select the hour, minutes, seconds or AM/PM in the Time edit box and type a new entry. (You can also select each component of the time and use the spinner arrows to change it.)

7. If you want to change the time zone, click the Time Zone tab to display this map:

Year 2000 ready

If you are concerned with how your computer will handle dates starting in the year 2000, you can relax. Windows 98 is prepared for the new millenium. You can set your computer so that it accepts year 2000 dates by double-clicking the Regional Settings icon in the Control Panel window and then displaying the Date tab. Click the arrows below When A Two Digit Year Is Entered setting to set the desired ending year. Bear in mind that the Year 2000 feature has a 100-year span (the default is 1930 to 2029).

8. Select the zone you want from the drop-down list.

9. Assuming you don't really want to change the date, time, and time zone, click Cancel to close the Date/Time Properties dialog box without making any changes.

You can change the date and time formats by double-clicking the Regional Settings icon in Control Panel to display the Regional Settings Properties dialog box. Selecting a region from a drop-down list on the Regional Settings tab changes the way programs display and sort numbers and currency, as well as dates and times. (Changing the region doesn't affect the language used in menus and dialog boxes.) You can also customize the display of these elements on the corresponding tabs of the dialog box. For example, if you prefer to display the day before the month in dates, you can click the Date tab. Then click the arrow to the right for the Long Date Style box, select *dddd, dd MMMM, yyyy* from the drop-down list, and click OK. (You can also customize the way Windows handles year-2000 dates on this tab; see the tip on the facing page.)

The Regional Settings icon

Changing the date display style

Adjusting the Mouse

You can change how fast you have to double-click the mouse button or make other adjustments to the mouse by using the Mouse icon in the Control Panel window. Here's how:

The Mouse icon

1. In the Control Panel window, double-click the Mouse icon to display this dialog box:

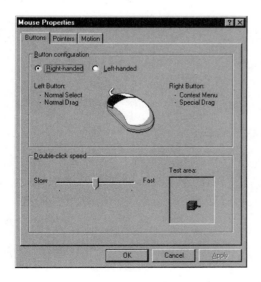

2. On the Double-Click Speed slider on the Buttons tab, drag the indicator to the left to slow down double-clicking, so that you can take more time between clicks and still have Windows recognize the action as a double-click.

3. Test your adjustment by double-clicking the Test Area jack-in-the-box. Jack jumps up when you double-click the box at the correct speed. (Double-click again to tuck Jack back in the box.)

4. Make any necessary adjustments to the speed, and when you are ready, click OK to close the dialog box.

You can also change the button configuration on the Buttons tab. If you are a southpaw and find it easier to click and highlight text with the right mouse button instead of the left, select the Left-Handed option in the Button Configuration section. The switch takes place as soon as you click OK. (Obviously, you then "right-click" with the left mouse button to display a shortcut menu.)

If the Windows 98 Mouse Pointers component is installed on your computer, you can click the Pointers tab of the Mouse Properties dialog box and select a different set, or scheme, of pointers. You can even design your own scheme by selecting an event in the list box, then clicking the Browse button, selecting a pointer to represent the event, and clicking Open. When you have specified pointers for all the events in the list box, you can save the scheme by clicking the Save As button and naming the set.

On the Motion tab of the Mouse Properties dialog box, you can change the pointer speed and have the mouse pointer leave a trail so that you can see it more easily as you move it across the screen.

Adjusting the Keyboard

If your keyboard repeats characters too fast or if the insertion point blinks too fast or too slow, you can make adjustments in the Keyboard Properties dialog box. Let's experiment:

The Keyboard icon

1. Double-click the Keyboard icon in the Control Panel window to display this dialog box:

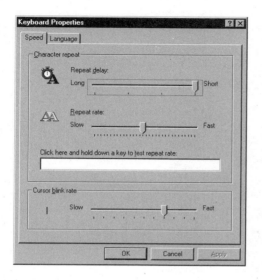

2. The Repeat Delay slider determines how long Windows waits before starting to repeat a key you are holding down. Drag the indicator all the way to the left to make the repeat delay as long as possible.

Adjusting the repeat delay

3. The Repeat Rate slider determines how rapidly Windows repeats the key after the initial delay. Drag the indicator all the way to the left to make the repeat rate as slow as possible.

Adjusting the repeat rate

4. Test your changes by clicking an insertion point in the Click Here edit box below the Repeat Rate slider and holding down any character key. As you'll see, Windows now responds very slowly to this keyboard action.

5. Adjust the Repeat Delay and Repeat Rate sliders until you find a speed to suit your typing style.

6. If you want, change the cursor blink rate by adjusting the slider at the bottom of the dialog box.

Adjusting the cursor blink rate

7. Click OK to implement your changes, or click Cancel to discard them.

The Accessibility Options icon

Accommodating Different Abilities

If you have a physical condition that makes using the computer difficult, you might want to check out the Accessibility Options icon in the Control Panel window. Double-clicking this icon displays the dialog box shown here:

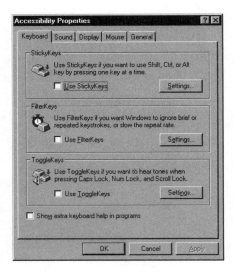

The Accessibility Wizard

If you need to adjust vision, sound, or mobility settings to use the computer, you may want to use the Accessibility Wizard which helps you determine what options to set. To access this wizard, click the Start button, point to Programs, Accessories, and Accessibility, and then click Accessibility Wizard. (If the wizard is not listed, you may need to install it. See page 154 for more information on installing Windows components.) In the first dialog box, you select your text size preference. Once you make your selection, the wizard takes you through other dialog boxes that allow you to adjust the appropriate settings. You can also set the amount of idle time before the computer reverts back to its default settings. (This feature is especially useful when there are several people using the same computer.) To undo any accessibility settings you make, you can change the settings by double-clicking the Accessibility Options icon in Control Panel. If you changed your text size preference, you need to work through the wizard again to change your preference.

Among other options, this multi-tabbed dialog box allows you to specify the following:

- **StickyKeys.** You can press the Ctrl, Alt, or Shift key and have the key remain active until you press a key other than Ctrl, Alt, or Shift. This feature is designed for people who have difficulty pressing more than one key at a time.

- **FilterKeys.** You can instruct the computer to ignore accidental or repeated keystrokes. (As you saw in the previous section, you can also adjust the keyboard repeat rate to avoid this problem.)

- **ToggleKeys.** The computer will emit one tone when you turn on the Caps Lock, Scroll Lock, or Num Lock key and another tone when you turn any of these keys off.

- **SoundSentry.** You can specify that a part of the screen flashes whenever your computer makes a sound.

- **ShowSounds.** You can tell the programs you use to display text captions or informative icons for any sounds they make.

- **High Contrast.** You can tell Windows to use colors and fonts that make the screen easier to read. (You can also tailor the display yourself, as we discussed on page 156.)

- **MouseKeys.** You can commandeer the numeric keypad to control your mouse pointer.

- **SerialKeys.** You can attach alternative devices to the computer's serial port if you have difficulty using a standard keyboard or mouse.

You might want to explore the various sections of this dialog box to get a feel for the many accessibility options that are available.

Adjusting Multimedia Devices

If you have multimedia accessories on your computer, such as a sound card and speakers, you can make adjustments to the setup by double-clicking the Multimedia icon in the Control Panel window to display this dialog box:

The Multimedia icon

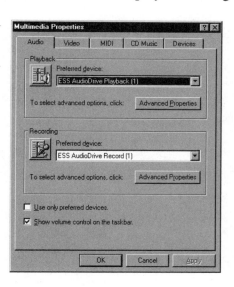

In the multi-tabbed Multimedia Properties dialog box, you can alter the audio, video, MIDI (for *Musical Instrument Digital Interface*), and CD Music properties, depending on

Microsoft Magnifier

If your eyesight is poor, you can use Microsoft Magnifier to make parts of your screen more legible. To start Microsoft Magnifier, you choose Programs, Accessories, Accessibility, and then Microsoft Magnifier from the Start menu. In the Microsoft Magnifier dialog box, you can change options that increase or decrease the magnification level, set tracking options, invert the display colors, and use High Contrast. Click OK to implement your changes. You can then point to objects on the regular screen to have them appear in a magnified window at the top of your screen. To close Microsoft Magnifier, click its button on the taskbar and click Exit.

which accessories are installed on your computer. You can also inspect and adjust your multimedia accessories on the Devices tab. Most likely, you won't need to make any adjustments in this dialog box. However, if you have a multimedia computer, you might want to take a look at the options.

The Sounds icon

If you have a sound card, you can use the Sounds icon in the Control Panel window to assign sounds to system and application events. Double-clicking this icon opens this dialog box:

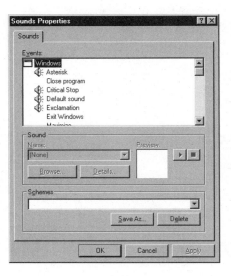

Previewing sounds

After you select an event from the list, select a sound from the Name drop-down list, or use the Browse button to locate a sound file you have created. You can "preview" a sound in the Preview section of the dialog box before you assign it.

Multimedia programs

To access Windows's multimedia programs, choose Programs, Accessories, and then Entertainment from the Start menu. You can use the programs on the Entertainment menu to play CDs and media clips, record sounds, and adjust your speaker volume. For more information, consult each program's Help menu.

DVD

DVD is a new form of compact disc currently used for movies. Windows 98 supports DVD playback. DVD-ROM drives which are used for storage, are also supported in Windows 98. For information about the hardware specifications and settings needed in order to use DVD, see Windows 98 Help.

You can control the volume of sounds by clicking the sound icon to the right of the clock on the taskbar to display a slider like this one:

Click the desktop to close the slider. Double-click the sound icon to display this more complex Volume Control dialog box:

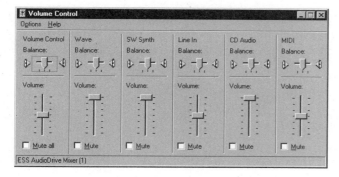

As you can see, if you know what you're doing, a variety of tools are available to help you coax maximum performance from your multimedia computer.

That concludes our quick tour of the Windows 98 customization options. As we said, you will probably want to experiment with the options you are allowed to change to discover the setup that best suits the way you work.

Web TV

Built into Windows 98 is a feature that enables you to view regular and interactive (or Web) TV on your computer. To activate this feature, you first need to install a TV tuner adapter card that is compatible with Windows 98. If you don't have a TV tuner adapter card but do have an Internet connection, you can still receive TV program listings by downloading them from a Web site. If you have neither a TV tuner adapter card nor an Internet connection but are on an intranet, you can receive video and other information from your network.

7

Solving Common Problems

We discuss the steps you can take to reduce potential problems to mild inconveniences. Included are discussions of backing up and restoring files; cleaning up hard drives, scanning them for errors, and defragmenting them; and troubleshooting startup problems.

Clean up a fragmented hard disk with Disk Defragmenter

Use ScanDisk to keep your hard disk in tip-top shape

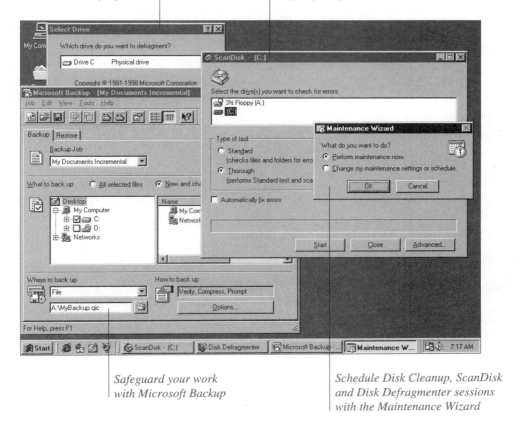

Safeguard your work with Microsoft Backup

Schedule Disk Cleanup, ScanDisk and Disk Defragmenter sessions with the Maintenance Wizard

In this chapter, we show you how to use some of the problem-solving tools that come with Windows 98. As you work your way through our examples, your goal is two-fold: first, you want to prevent problems to the extent possible; and second, you want to have a strategy in place for dealing with the problems that will inevitably occur. How well-prepared you are for these problems could make the difference between a minor inconvenience and a major catastrophe.

Many people have an aversion to thinking about problems before they happen. Others take Murphy's Law ("anything that can go wrong will go wrong") quite literally and build contingency plans into every undertaking. Between the optimists and the pessimists, the rest of us hope for the best and learn from experience. Unfortunately, learning from experience can be very painful (and expensive) where computers are concerned. Take our word for it: if you have important documents that would be difficult or time-consuming to reconstruct, a little time spent planning ahead will pay big dividends in the event of software or hardware misbehavior.

Backing Up Your Files

An effective plan for safeguarding your documents has two phases: first, and most obvious, take steps to avoid losing them, and second, back them up regularly so that they are easy to recover if you do make a mistake. You'll find some suggestions for general file safety in the adjacent tip. Here, we'll focus on backing up.

Backing up is like flossing your teeth or taking out the garbage: necessary, but not very exciting. It's easy to put it off. But we can't stress the point enough: sooner or later, something will go wrong, and you will lose valuable documents. Just as a bad dental checkup can induce people to start flossing, losing documents can, overnight, instill the habit of backing up.

The term *backing up* simply means making a copy of your documents that will be available in case you have problems with your computer. Storing copies safely off your computer can reduce disasters to mere inconveniences and make recov-

File-safety strategies

If you keep the following pointers in mind, you may never have to deal with lost documents:

- Windows sometimes displays a confirmation prompt when it wants you to think twice about a particular action. You should take these prompts seriously. It's easy to get in the habit of hitting Enter without really reading them.

- Delete documents to the Recycle Bin so that you can easily undelete them.

- Keep your folders and documents organized (see Chapter 3). As a general rule, don't keep copies of the same document in several different folders. If you work on one version of a document one day and on another version another day, you'll lose one set of changes. No program we know of can help you merge the changes so that they are all in one document.

- The most important way of safeguarding your documents is the easiest: save your work often.

ering your work a matter of simply transferring the copies from disks or tape. Taking some time to evaluate your needs and develop a simple and effective backup strategy can really pay off when the inevitable document loss occurs.

You can use regular or high-capacity disks, a tape drive, a removable hard drive, or another computer as the storage medium for backups. For our examples, we'll show you how to back up to regular floppy disks, but you'll easily be able to apply these techniques to other media. Windows provides two methods for backing up documents:

- **Copying.** The simplest way to back up just a few documents is to copy them using the techniques discussed on page 81.

Backing up a few documents

- **Using Microsoft Backup.** If you get to the point where you are backing up large numbers of documents or single documents that are larger than one disk, you will probably want to use the Backup program, which employs a special coding system to compress files as it copies them so that the files take up less space. You must then use the Restore component of Backup to restore the files back onto your hard disk in a usable format.

Backing up many documents

Remember way back when we told you to store all your data files in subfolders of the My Documents folder to make backing up easier? Now you'll see how this strategy pays off. In the following sections, you'll first create a full backup of the My Documents folder, then you'll create an incremental backup, which safeguards any additions or changes made since the last full backup. Finally, you'll see how to restore files.

Creating a Full Backup

To experiment with Backup, you need to have a couple of floppy disks handy. (You can use the disk you formatted in Chapter 3 and any other disk containing information you don't need.) Then follow these steps:

1. Click the Start button and choose Programs, Accessories, System Tools, and then Backup. (If Backup isn't on the System Tools submenu, it is probably not installed on your computer. To install the program, follow the instructions for

Starting Microsoft Backup

adding a Windows component on page 154. Backup can be found under System Tools in the Components list.)

2. If Backup displays this dialog box:

click No. (Backup has checked to see whether your computer has a tape drive. If it has one, Backup assumes you will use that drive for backing up.) You then see this dialog box:

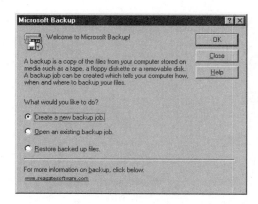

3. Click OK to accept the default Create A New Backup Job selection. Backup then displays the first Backup Wizard dialog box, shown here:

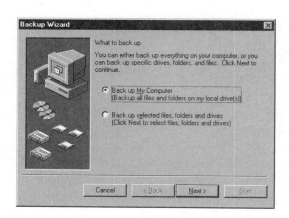

4. You just want to back up the My Documents folder on the hard drive, so click the second option and then click Next to display this dialog box:

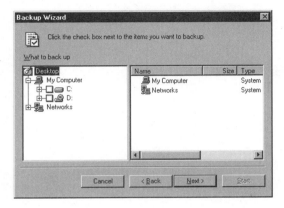

As you can see, this dialog box looks very similar to the Windows Explorer window, and you display folder contents in the left and right panes the same way you do in Windows Explorer (see page 63).

5. Double-click the C drive icon in the left pane to expand the diagram in the left pane.

6. Click the check box beside the My Documents folder in the left pane to indicate that you want to back up all the documents in this folder and its subfolders. The window now looks like this:

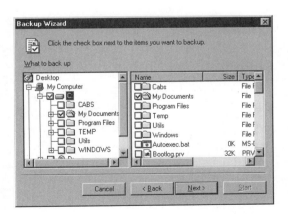

My Computer backups

If you have access to a high-capacity backup device (floppy disks are not practical for this purpose), you can use Microsoft Backup to back up all the files on your hard drive, including the registry files that your computer needs to work properly. If you take the time to copy your entire system to a safe place (such as a tape drive or removable hard drive), you can restore your system in the event of a catastrophe by following the steps on page 189. To back up My Computer, simply select that option in the Backup Wizard's first dialog box.

7. Click Next to display the next Backup Wizard dialog box, where you specify what files you want to back up. Because this is the first time you have backed up this folder and because you want to do a full backup, simply select the All Selected Files option and then click the Next button to display the dialog box shown here:

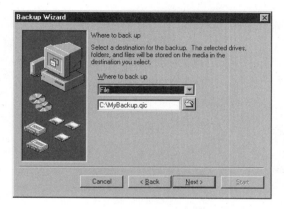

8. Next, insert a disk in your floppy drive, and then change the backup location by clicking the folder button to display this dialog box:

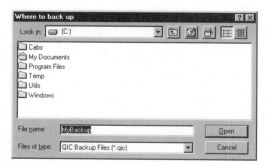

Comparing files

To ensure that backup files exactly match the corresponding original files, Backup compares them. To speed up the backup job, you can click the Options button at the bottom of the Backup window, deselect the Compare Original And Backup Files check box on the General tab, and click OK. However, you then run the risk that your backup files won't restore correctly, and usually accuracy is more important than time.

9. Click the Up One Level button, double-click your floppy drive, and then click Open to update the storage location in the Backup Wizard's dialog box. Then click Next to display the dialog box shown on the facing page.

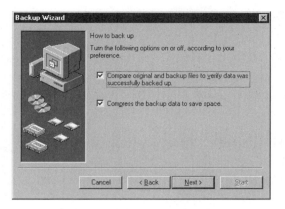

10. Here, you select your backup preferences. Leave both options selected and click Next to display the final wizard dialog box:

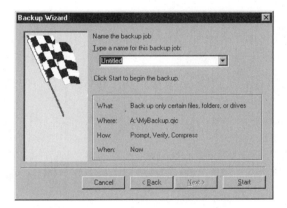

11. Type *My Documents Full* as the name for the backup job. Then click Start. Backup goes to work, seeking out and backing up the selected files and displaying its progress on the screen. If you were backing up a large group of files, Backup would prompt you each time it needed you to insert a new disk.

12. When you see the Operation completed message, click OK. Backup then reports how many files and bytes it backed up, how long the backup operation took, and the extent to which it compressed the files. After reading the information, click OK to return to the Microsoft Backup window.

Using filters

Suppose one of your project folders contains 20 documents that you are actively working on. The program associated with those documents retains the previous versions of the files every time you save them by appending a hidden BAK extension to the file names. When you back up your work using Microsoft Backup, you want to safeguard the current documents but you don't want to take up space with all the BAK files. To exclude them from the backup operation, start Microsoft Backup, click the Options button, click the Exclude tab, and click the Add button. Click Custom Type, type *BAK* in the edit box, and click OK. (You can exclude many file types by selecting their extensions from the Registered Type list in the Add/Exclude dialog box.) Click OK again to return to the Microsoft Backup window, where you can select the project folder whose files you want to back up. Even though the entire folder is selected, the BAK files will not be backed up.

Creating an Incremental Backup

Suppose you want to do a full backup of your My Documents folder every Friday, but on Monday, Tuesday, Wednesday, and Thursday, you want to back up only the files that have changed during the day. Here's how to create a backup job that will accomplish this task:

1. On the Backup tab of the Microsoft Backup window, display the contents of the C drive and make sure that the My Documents folder is selected in the left pane.

2. Click the Options button at the bottom of the dialog box, click the Type tab, and click the New And Changed Files Only option. The dialog box looks like this:

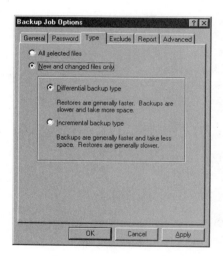

As you have seen, selecting All Selected Files creates a full backup of all the files in the My Documents folder and its sub-folders. Selecting New And Changed Files Only gives you two additional options: differential backup, which backs up files that have changed since the last full backup; and incre-mental backup, which backs up files that have changed since the previous incremental backup, or since the last full backup if there have been no intervening incremental backups.

Differential vs. incremental
backups

3. Select the Incremental Backup Type option and click OK.

4. Choose Save As from the Job menu, type *My Documents Incremental* as the job name, and click Save.

5. Insert a different floppy disk, and in the Microsoft Backup window, click Start. Then click OK twice to return to the Microsoft Backup window.

6. Close the Microsoft Backup window.

Now you label five disks with the days of the work week, and on Monday through Thursday, you back up the additions and changes to the My Documents folder. Simply insert that day's disk, select Open An Existing Backup Job in the Microsoft Backup welcome window, click OK, and double-click My Documents Incremental in the Open Backup Job window. On Friday, you back up the entire folder with the Friday disk and the My Documents Full procedure.

Restoring Documents

If Murphy's Law proves correct, you will at some point need to restore files from disk. Let's give the restoration process a dry run. For the next example, you need to simulate the accidental deletion of the documents from the Staff Party subfolder of My Documents by changing the name of the folder, like this:

1. Double-click the My Documents folder on the desktop to open its folder window.

2. Rename the Staff Party folder as *Party*. Then close the My Documents window.

Now the Staff Party folder is "gone." Let's restore it and its contents from the backup disk you just created:

1. Insert the disk you used for the full backup.

2. Start Microsoft Backup and when you see the welcome window shown earlier on page 184, click Restore Backed Up Files and click OK. Backup starts the Restore Wizard, which displays the dialog box shown on the next page.

Adjusting backup jobs

If you want to back up a set of files that is almost, but not quite, the same as one specified by a backup job you have already created, you can open the file set in the Backup window and then adjust the selections to tailor the file set for this particular backup operation. If you don't save the new job, when you click the Start button, Backup prompts you to save the job with the new settings. Clicking Yes overwrites the old settings and starts the backup operation. Clicking No stops the process. If you want to retain the original settings, make the changes and then choose Save As from the Job menu to save the new settings as a different backup job.

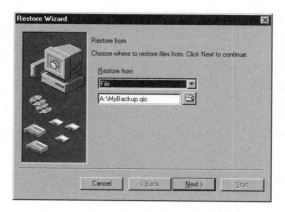

3. Click Next to restore files from the disk in your floppy drive. The wizard displays this dialog box:

4. Click OK. You see this dialog box:

Restore options

Clicking the Options button on the Restore tab of the Backup window displays a set of options for tailoring the restore operation. On the General tab, you can specify what to do when restoring files that already exist. On the Report tab, you can determine what information is reported after the restore job. To determine whether files should be restored to their original location or to an alternative location, use the Where To Restore section of the Backup window.

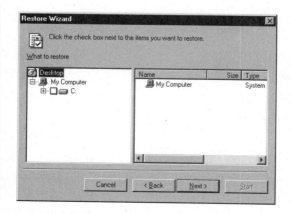

5. Double-click the C icon and then the My Documents icon, click the Staff Party check box to select it, and click Next.

6. Click Next to restore the Staff Party folder to its original location and to display this dialog box:

7. Because you are not replacing any files, simply click Start. Then click OK to accept the media selection. Backup restores the Staff Party folder and all its files from your backup disk.

8. Click OK twice. Then close the Microsoft Backup window and remove the disk from your floppy drive.

9. Double-click the My Documents icon on the desktop. As you can see, the folder now contains a Staff Party subfolder as well as the renamed Party subfolder.

10. Close all open windows.

From this simple demonstration, you can see how easily you can recover files in the event of a catastrophe, but only if you have taken the time to back up your documents.

Optimizing Your Hard Disk

The risk of experiencing disk and file problems is greatly reduced if you regularly optimize your hard disk. In this context, optimization entails routinely deleting obsolete files, checking the integrity of your hard drive and file structure, and defragmenting the disk. We'll briefly cover these optimization procedures here, and then we'll show you how to use the Maintenance Wizard to automate these tasks.

Scheduling backups

Windows 98 can help you remember to perform any of a number of critical tasks on a regular basis with its Task Scheduler program. For example, you can use it to schedule backups. To do so, you either double-click My Computer and open the Scheduled Tasks folder, or choose Programs, Accessories, System Tools, and then Scheduled Tasks from the Start menu. Double-click Add Scheduled Task at the top of the list to open its wizard, select Backup in the list of applications to open, and click Next. Enter a name for the task and specify the Weekly option to tell Windows how often it should run this program. In the wizard's next dialog box, select the weekday and the time you want Backup to start, and then click Next. (You must enter a time when you will be present, because Windows will open the first Backup dialog box and then wait for you to choose a backup job and click OK to have Backup perform its task.) In the final dialog box, click the Open Advanced Properties check box and then click Finish so that you can fine-tune this task on the Settings and Schedule tabs of the Backup dialog box. Once you have created a task, you can right-click it and choose Properties from the shortcut menu to alter its settings.

Using Disk Cleanup

Back in Chapter 3, we showed you how to view the properties of your computer's C drive, and you may have noticed a Disk Cleanup button in the drive's Properties dialog box (see page 61). Clicking that button displays a Disk Cleanup dialog box, which lists files that have been created behind the scenes but that neither you nor your computer are likely to need again. You can have Disk Cleanup delete the files to regain space on your hard drive. Here's how to access Disk Cleanup by a more direct route:

1. Choose Programs, Accessories, System Tools, and then Disk Cleanup from the Start menu. You see this dialog box:

2. Click OK to clean up your C drive. Disk Cleanup does a quick survey of the drive and then displays this dialog box:

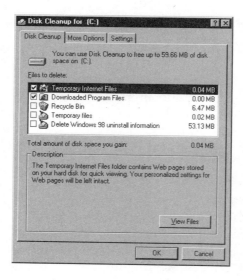

3. Click the Recycle Bin and Temporary Files check boxes, click OK, and then click Yes to confirm the deletions. Disk Cleanup goes to work, freeing up space on your hard drive.

Using ScanDisk

The information in a document is not necessarily stored in one chunk but may be scattered throughout your hard disk, which is divided into allocation units (sometimes called *clusters*), each with its own number. When you save a document, Windows stores it in the first available allocation unit and uses a sort of address book called the *file allocation table*, or *FAT*, to keep track of the unit in which the first part of the document is stored. When the unit is full, Windows looks for the next unit and records its number, and so on, until the entire file is saved.

The file allocation table (FAT)

For the most part, this system works pretty well, but occasionally problems arise that can lead to loss of data. You can minimize the chances of such problems by regularly running ScanDisk to check for the following conditions:

- Bad (damaged) disk sectors

Bad sectors

- Data on the disk that doesn't have an entry in the FAT, a condition known as *lost file fragments*

Lost file fragments

- Two files that have been assigned to the same allocation unit, a condition known as *cross-linked files*

Cross-linked files

- Problems involving long file names, your folder structure, or compressed disks (see the tip on page 195)

File name, folder structure, or compressed disk problems

ScanDisk options

Clicking the Options button in the ScanDisk window displays a dialog box in which you can tailor the disk surface scan part of the Thorough option. You can restrict the surface scan to a specific area of the disk, and you can restrict the test to reading sectors, instead of both reading and writing. You can also prevent ScanDisk from moving any hidden and system files that are stored in bad sectors. (Some programs may get confused if they expect to find these files in specific places.)

Automatic ScanDisk

If your computer is shut down improperly or if your hard disk suffers some sort of physical injury, Windows 98 automatically runs ScanDisk to check your hard drive's condition. It corrects any files that have been damaged and regains any empty disk space.

Lost fragments

If ScanDisk finds a lost file fragment, it converts it to a file and then stores the file with a name like FILE0000. You can view the file to see if it contains anything worth salvaging before deleting it. If you don't want to examine the lost-fragment files, you can select Free in the Lost File Fragments section of the dialog box that appears when you click Advanced in the ScanDisk window. ScanDisk then simply frees up the space occupied by the file fragments on your disk.

To keep your hard disk(s) in tip-top shape, you can tell Scan-Disk to detect and then repair or work around any problems it finds. Here's how:

1. Close any open programs (ScanDisk runs faster this way). Then choose Programs, Accessories, System Tools, and ScanDisk from the Start menu to display this window:

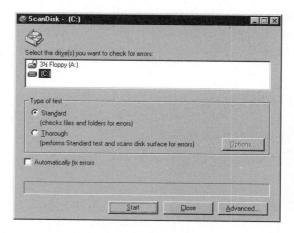

As you can see, you can use ScanDisk to fix problems on hard disk(s) and floppy disks, but not CD-ROMs.

Selecting a drive to scan

2. Be sure (C:) is selected in the list of drives, select Thorough in the Type Of Test section, check that the Automatically Fix Errors check box is deselected, and click Start. ScanDisk goes to work, reporting its progress in a bar at the bottom of the dialog box. (The disk surface scan may take a few minutes.)

3. If ScanDisk finds no problems, it displays a ScanDisk Results dialog box like this one:

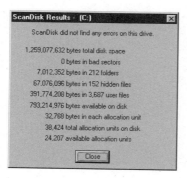

After reading the information in the dialog box, you can click Close to close it.

4. If ScanDisk finds a problem, it reports it in a dialog box, in which you can select options to specify how you want the problem handled. (In some dialog boxes, you can click a More Info button if you don't know how to proceed.) Select the option you want and then click OK.

If you select Automatically Fix Errors before clicking Start, ScanDisk corrects any problems it finds. How it fixes them depends on the specifications in the ScanDisk Advanced Options dialog box, which is displayed when you click Advanced in the bottom right corner of the ScanDisk window:

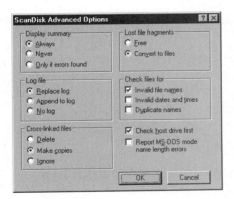

Here, you can specify whether ScanDisk should display a summary of fixed errors and how it should handle its log. You can also specify the method for fixing cross-linked files and lost clusters, what file elements should be checked, and whether to check a host drive before a compressed drive.

Using Disk Defragmenter

Windows comes with a program called Disk Defragmenter. Because of the way Windows stores files, your hard disk can be a checkerboard of full and empty allocation units. Disk Defragmenter uses the FAT to find the scattered parts of each file and stores the parts in a contiguous group of allocation units. Working with a program or document is then easier because its file is stored in one place, and Windows doesn't have to jump all over your hard disk to put the file together.

Compressing disks

Windows includes DriveSpace, a compression utility that squeezes more storage space out of a disk. You should first use the other methods described in this chapter, because DriveSpace is not for the fainthearted. You must be diligent about backing up a compressed disk to avoid the risk of corruption and loss of data. You can compress your hard disk(s), floppy disks, or the free space on your hard drive. Your disk will be physically the same; the files on it are compressed, not the disk itself. (Compressed free space is not smaller; the space is set up to compress anything new stored there.) A coding system reduces the number of characters in the files, which are crammed into a master file, called a *compressed volume file* (CVF). The CVF is hidden on an uncompressed part of the disk, which is designated the *host drive*. Never move or mess with the CVF! You can use programs and create documents as before—DriveSpace does the work behind the scenes. To compress a disk, choose Programs, Accessories, System Tools, and then DriveSpace from the Start menu. Select the drive and choose Compress from the Drive menu, or choose Create Empty from the Advanced menu to compress free space. Then click Start. Drive-Space may restart your computer. When the program is finished, it tells you how much space your drive has. To decompress a drive, follow the same steps, but choose Uncompress from the Drive menu.

Before running Disk Defragmenter, you should use ScanDisk as we just described to fix any FAT problems that might exist on your hard disk. A complete discussion of the defragmentation program's options is beyond the scope of this book, but here are the basic steps involved:

1. With no other programs open, click the Start button and choose Programs, Accessories, System Tools, and then Disk Defragmenter. You see this dialog box:

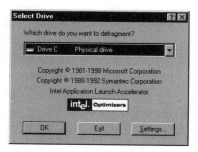

Selecting a drive to defragment

2. With Drive C selected in the drop-down list box, click OK. Disk Defragmenter then starts defragmenting the C drive, reporting its progress as it goes along. (Like ScanDisk, this process can take several minutes.)

Displaying the details

If you click the Show Details button, Defragmenter displays a graphic representation of file fragments being assembled into complete files. (To get a better understanding of what each color-coded box means, click the Legend button.) To close this window, simply click Hide Details. You can also stop or pause the defragmentation process by clicking their respective buttons.

Which disks can be defragmented?

Disk Defragmenter works with local hard disks and floppy disks, but not with network disks. It can handle disks that have been compressed using DriveSpace (see the tip on the previous page), but not disks that have been compressed with other compression programs.

3. When the defragmentation process is complete, you see this message box:

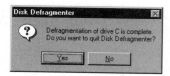

4. Click Yes to quit the program.

If your disk was severely fragmented, you'll notice that operations requiring hard disk access take less time than before.

Using the Maintenance Wizard

You have seen how to use Disk Cleanup, ScanDisk, and Disk Defragmenter to spruce up your hard drive and optimize its performance. With the Maintenance Wizard, you can schedule these tasks to be performed on a regular basis, perhaps during non-working hours when these housekeeping chores won't interfere with your other tasks. Here's how to set up the Maintenance Wizard:

1. Choose Programs, Accessories, System Tools, and then Maintenance Wizard from the Start menu. The first time you use the Wizard, it displays this dialog box first:

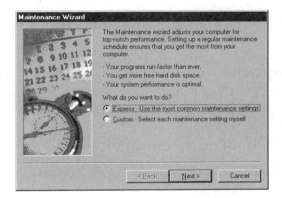

2. Click Next to accept the default option, and click Next again to select the default Night schedule. This dialog box appears:

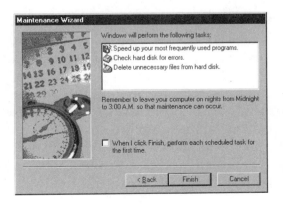

Changing maintenance settings

To customize your maintenance settings after you've first used the Maintenance Wizard, access the wizard as described on this page, and click the Change option in the first dialog box. In the next dialog box, click Custom instead of Express, and the wizard will guide you through the necessary steps.

3. Click Finish. The wizard may display this dialog box:

4. Click No to close the dialog box. (See the adjacent tip for information about FAT32.)

Because you have scheduled the Maintenance Wizard to work its magic at night, you will obviously have to leave your computer on at night, or the maintenance work won't get done. If you forget and turn off your machine for the night, you can choose the Maintenance Wizard from the Start menu at any time. You see this dialog box:

Simply click OK to run the maintenance programs, bearing in mind that they might take a while.

Troubleshooting Startup Problems

If your computer doesn't start, or boot, properly when you turn it on, the glitch could be traceable to any number of problems that are way beyond the scope of this book. For the most part, you are probably better off calling in an expert than trying to sort things out on your own. However, one or two tricks of the trade might help you solve the problem yourself. At the very least, you might be able to retrieve any critical files that you have failed to back up, before someone starts dissecting your machine. And if you know all about MS-DOS and its utilities, you may be able to go beyond the information we provide here and get everything working again.

FAT32

With Windows 98, you can use an improved version of the file allocation table called *FAT32* instead of the traditional FAT. The advantages are that a disk that is larger than 2 GB can be formatted as one disk, and storage is more efficient because FAT32 uses smaller clusters than the traditional FAT. If you are an experienced computer user, you can convert your hard disk to FAT32 by choosing Programs, Accessories, System Tools, and Drive Converter (FAT32) from the Start menu. Windows then walks you through the process using the Drive Converter Wizard. Be sure to back up critical files and to create a Windows 98 Emergency Startup Disk before performing this conversion (see the facing page). You can't revert to the traditional FAT once you have made the conversion, unless you reformat the FAT32 drive. If you want more information about FAT32, consult Windows 98 Help.

Creating a Startup Disk

A startup disk is a floppy disk that can be used to start your computer if for some reason it decides to play dead. (The likelihood that you will ever use the disk is slim, but if you have to call in an expert, he or she might ask you for it.) A startup disk might have been created for your computer when Windows 98 was installed. If for some reason you don't have that disk, you can create one now by following these steps:

1. Choose Settings and then Control Panel from the Start menu.

2. Double-click the Add/Remove Programs icon and click the Startup Disk tab to display these options:

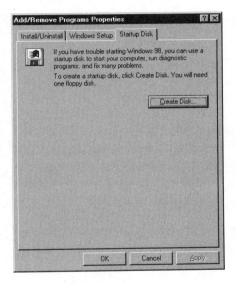

3. Click the Create Disk button and then follow the prompts, inserting your Windows 98 CD-ROM and a floppy disk when requested.

4. Click OK to close the dialog box.

Starting from the Startup Menu

Windows 98 has some useful programs that can help you solve startup problems, but to use them, you have to be able to get your computer up and running. One way to goad your computer into action is to start it using your Windows 98 startup disk, but don't bother doing this unless you are familiar

Automatic Skip Driver

One of Windows little helpers is Automatic Skip Driver. This program works behind the scenes to identify device failures that have caused Windows 98 to stop responding on startup. It marks problematic devices so that they will be bypassed on subsequent startups, and maintains a history of devices in a file called ASD.log. To manually run Automatic Skip Driver, choose Run from the Start menu and then type *asd* in the Open edit box. If no errors have occurred, a message tells you that no critical operation failures were reported. If an error did occur, you can click Details in the dialog box that appears, to identify the failing device and see a suggestion about how to address the problem.

enough with MS-DOS commands to move around your drives and run programs. Otherwise, follow these steps:

1. Turn on your computer, and when you see the instruction to press a key to run Setup, press the Ctrl key or the F8 key to display the Microsoft Windows 98 Startup Menu, which lists several choices. (You may have to try this step a couple of times to test which key works with your computer and when you should press it to make the menu appear.)

2. Enter the number that goes with your selection, as follows:

• **Normal.** Windows will boot as usual.

• **Logged.** Windows will write down everything that happens during startup so that an expert can see what might be causing the problem.

• **Safe Mode.** Windows will start itself using the simplest hardware configuration (no fancy video drivers, no network, no CD-ROM drive, no printer, and so on).

• **Step-By-Step Confirmation.** Windows will display each command in the startup procedure before running it. You press Y to run the command and N to skip it. If Windows can't run the command, you see an error message, which might help you narrow down the cause of the problem.

• **Command Prompt Only.** Windows will start its version of the MS-DOS operating system.

• **Safe Mode Command Prompt Only.** Windows will start MS-DOS using the simplest hardware configuration.

• **Previous Version Of MS-DOS.** Windows will start the version of MS-DOS that previously ran on your computer (presumably successfully).

Checking Your Files

If you are able to start Windows 98 with any of the first four options, you might want to run the System File Checker to test your operating system files. Here's how:

1. Choose Programs, Accessories, System Tools, and System File Checker from the Start menu to display this dialog box:

Starting System File Checker

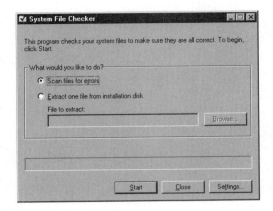

If System File Checker does not appear on the System Tools menu, open Windows Explorer, navigate to the C:\Windows\-System folder, and double-click the *sfc* program file to start the program.

2. Click the Start button.

3. If System File Checker finds any Windows 98 files that are corrupted or missing, it asks whether to back up existing versions before replacing them with the original files from your installation disks.

4. When System File Checker finishes its audit, click Details in its message box to see this report:

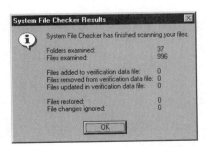

5. Click OK twice, and then click Close to quit System File Checker.

Using the Startup Troubleshooter

Windows 98 Help has a useful tool for diagnosing startup (and shutdown) problems. Follow these steps to take a look:

1. Choose Help from the Start menu, click the Index tab, type *startup* in the edit box, and double-click *troubleshooting* in the topic list. Then simply click the *Click here* link to start the troubleshooter. The Help window now looks like this:

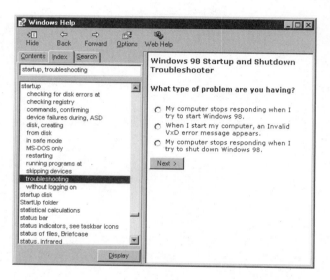

2. Click your way through the troubleshooter, as appropriate for your particular problem.

   With any luck, these simple procedures will help you fix whatever is ailing Windows 98. For more complex problems, you may have to call your computer's manufacturer or Microsoft for technical support, or visit your local repair shop.

   That's it for this chapter on problem-solving. Hopefully, being aware of the potential problems we've discussed will help you avoid them altogether and make your time at the computer more productive.

   Congratulations! You have now completed your Quick Course in Windows 98. By now, you should feel comfortable with most of the components of Windows. With the basics you have learned here, together with the Help feature, you can explore on your own how to best make Windows 98 work for you.

Index

Take the
whole family
siteseeing!

For Microsoft® Windows® 95 and Windows NT®

The Reference for Everyday Use in Home, School, and Office

1998 Edition Regular Online Updates

Official
Microsoft Bookshelf®
Internet Directory

Searchable on CD-ROM—with direct links to thousands of the best and most useful Internet sites

Microsoft *Press*

U.S.A.	**$39.99**
U.K.	£37.49 [V.A.T. included]
Canada	$55.99
ISBN 1-57231-617-9	

Want to update your stock portfolio? Explore space? Recognize consumer fraud? Find a better job? Trace your family tree? Research your term paper? Make bagels? Well, go for it! The OFFICIAL MICROSOFT® BOOK-SHELF® INTERNET DIRECTORY, 1998 EDITION, gives you reliable, carefully selected, up-to-date reviews of thousands of the Internet's most useful, entertaining, and functional Web sites. The searchable companion CD-ROM gives you direct, instant links to the sites in the book—a simple click of the mouse takes you wherever you want to go!

Developed jointly by Microsoft Press and the Microsoft Bookshelf product team, the OFFICIAL MICROSOFT BOOK-SHELF INTERNET DIRECTORY, 1998 EDITION, is updated regularly on the World Wide Web to keep you informed of our most current list of recommended sites. Microsoft Internet Explorer 4.0 is also included on the CD-ROM.

Microsoft *Press*

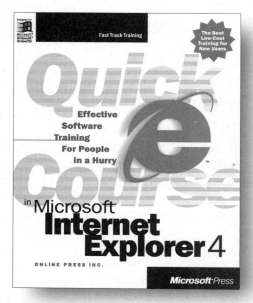